Cater Your Own Wedding

Easy Ways to
Do It Yourself in Style

By
Michael Flowers and Donna Bankhead

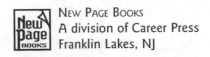
NEW PAGE BOOKS
A division of Career Press
Franklin Lakes, NJ

CATER YOUR OWN WEDDING
Cover design by Cheryl Finbow
Typesetting by Eileen Munson
Printed in the U.S.A. by Book-mart Press

To order this title, please call toll-free 1-800-CAREER-1 (NJ and Canada: 201-848-0310) to order using VISA or MasterCard, or for further information on books from Career Press.

The Career Press, Inc., 3 Tice Road, PO Box 687
Franklin Lakes, NJ 07417
www.careerpress.com

Library of Congress Cataloging-in-Publication Data

Flowers, Michael.
     Cater your own wedding : easy ways to do it yourself in style / by Michael Flowers and Donna Bankhead.
         p.   cm.
     Includes index.
     ISBN 1-56414-474-7 (pbk.)
     1. Weddings—United States—Planning. 2. Caterers and catering—United States. I. Bankhead, Donna. II. Title.

HQ745 .F58 2000
395.2'2--dc21   00-032883

「 ✒ 」

To the most

important

people in our

lives.

Melanie and Jonathan
—MCF

Bill, Emily, Chance, and Abby
—DAB

Acknowledgments

Although only two authors' names appear on the cover of this book, a number of other people made huge contributions to the finished product you hold in your hands. Linda Setzer, a writer for the *Hickory News* in Hickory, North Carolina, gave Mike the push and encouragement he needed to put his ideas down on paper and write the booklet that initiated this entire project. Becky Beus, an artist in Boise, Idaho, and one of the best cheerleaders a person could have, created all of the illustrations in this book. Our heartfelt gratitude goes to both of these wonderful women for their talent, insight, and friendship.

The contributions our families made to the writing of this book can't be understated. They stood behind us for a year and offered their love and support as we dealt with the long hours, hard work, and frustrations of collaborating on a book from opposite sides of the continent. We will always be grateful for their unselfishness in allowing us to reach for our dreams.

And finally, I'd like to thank Mike for his willingness to take a risk and let me in on his wonderful idea. After stumbling across his original booklet on his Website (*www.chefmike.com*), I barged right into his life and asked him to share his brainchild with me. I'll always be thankful that he didn't dismiss me as a cyberstalker and that he allowed me to be a part of this project.

Donna A. Bankhead

Contents

Introduction

If you are like most brides and have started making plans, you're discovering just how expensive a wedding can be. Adding up the cost of your wedding dress, the flowers, the photographer, and those little white bottles full of wedding bubbles, your budget can quickly spin out of control. And if you've met with any caterers for an estimate, you're probably realizing that you could buy a car—or at least make a healthy down payment on one—for the amount of money you'll spend on food!

Depending on your area of the country, a bare-bones, no-frills reception menu will run $12 to $18 per person. If you want to serve a full sit-down meal with alcoholic beverages, you're looking at up to $75 (sometimes more) per person. That's just for the meal; it doesn't include your costs to rent the reception facility, decorate, or provide entertainment. With a guest list of 200, you can spend anywhere from $3600 for a finger-sandwiches-and-fruit-trays reception to $15,000 for a prime-rib-with-all-the-trimmings meal.

Do you really want to let your
wedding guests eat your car?

With *Cater Your Own Wedding*, you don't have to. You can provide anything from a simple finger-foods buffet to a full-meal spread for a fraction of the cost a caterer would charge. All you need is this book and some reliable friends who are willing to give a few hours of their time. Much more than a cookbook for crowds, *Cater Your Own Wedding* is a comprehensive handbook that takes you (or whomever you recruit to organize and oversee the reception) through every step of planning, preparing, and putting on the reception.

Cater Your Own Wedding outlines several types of receptions including the Basic, Elegant, Ultimate, Brunch, Backyard Barbecue, and Dessert Receptions. Several menu options are given for each plan, and all menus within a particular plan have comparable preparation requirements. The plans can be customized to accommodate virtually any number of guests, as adaptations for a variety of serving quantities are provided for each recipe. Because few people have access to commercial kitchens and their large-scale cooking capacity, the recipes are broken down into portions that are manageable in any home kitchen. In addition, each plan details how many helpers the bride will need to recruit and each person's specific responsibilities. The entire reception is choreographed with down-to-the-minute timelines provided for each helper. To take even more guesswork out of the process, diagrams are included for arranging everything from relish trays to the wedding cake table to the reception hall.

This is just the beginning. Other topics *Cater Your Own Wedding* addresses include:

- Calculating how much food will be needed for the number of people expected.

- Shopping lists for each menu.

- Sanitation and food-care information.

- Checklists of items the bride may need to rent or borrow (such as tables and chairs, silver trays, linens, and ice containers).

- Step-by-step instructions on operating rented equipment such as chafing dishes and punch fountains.

- Table and hall decorating ideas.

Planning a wedding is stressful enough without having to decide which you want more—a knock-'em-dead reception or money to live on after the honeymoon. With *Cater Your Own Wedding,* you can have both.

First Things First

Your friends will think you're nuts. You're up to your eyeballs in wedding plans, and now you want to cater your own reception. They probably picture you racing around the kitchen an hour before the ceremony, stirring Swedish meatball sauce with one hand and applying mascara with the other while your mother tries to paint your toenails and your dad hyperventilates about getting to the church on time.

Tell your friends to relax.

The *Cater Your Own Wedding* definition of self-catering is not, "The bride slaves over a hot oven for weeks and shows up at the wedding with singed eyebrows and barbecue sauce under her fingernails." By following any of the reception plans in this book, you won't have much more to do than you would if you hired a professional caterer. You'll find the particulars later in this chapter, but in a nutshell, your only responsibilities are to choose the menu; recruit a group of friends to undertake specific parts of the reception; buy, rent, or borrow any furniture or equipment required for your plan; order your wedding cake; and splurge on something extravagant during your honeymoon with the money you saved by catering your own reception!

While organizing a spectacular shindig using one of the plans in this book is a pretty simple matter, you'll need more than just a great menu and knockout recipes. Menus and recipes are important when you're planning your reception, but you have to make sure your particular situation is right for a self-catered reception as well. The two most important factors in determining whether self-catering will work for you are your circle of family and friends and your reception site.

Your Circle of Family and Friends

Self-catering requires a group effort. Are your friends and loved ones willing to roll up their sleeves for you for a few hours? Depending on the reception plan you choose, you'll need anywhere from eight to 29 helpers. (Because the members of your wedding party—your bridesmaids, the groom's mother, and so forth—will be almost as busy as you are in the days before the wedding, think of other people who would agree to be on your reception team.)

Now, eight to 29 people may sound like a huge number of helpers to round up, but don't let that scare you away from a do-it-yourself reception. Most of your friends will be excited and honored that you asked them to be a part of your big day—especially when they see how simple the job you're asking them to do is. And don't forget about your fiancé's network of family and friends. His side of the aisle will be just as honored to be a part of the festivities as yours will.

Another thing to remember is that you may not actually have to *ask* as many people as your plan requires. Do you have friends or family members who belong to a cooking club or who love to cook? They may be able to recruit some of their fellow culinary artists to take on several (if not all) of the tasks for your reception. Many of the tasks in the reception plans call for two people to work together as a team. Because most of the menu items are simple to prepare (who can't make a pot of coffee or cut up vegetables?), a husband-and-wife team or a couple of roommates can easily handle them, reducing by half the number of people you'll need to recruit. You can also find one person for each job and let them fill out their team with their own friends or people they feel comfortable working with.

As you put your list of potential helpers together, a word of caution: Be sure to choose *reliable* friends, not just those who know their way around a kitchen. Your old college roommate may be able to turn a can of Vienna sausages into a reason for living, but if she's always breaking her promises or backing out of commitments at the last minute, move on to the next person on your list. A creative excuse will do little to relieve your guests' hunger pangs if she's in charge of making the main dish and decides to go on a Caribbean cruise the day before your wedding.

The Reception Site

You've found the perfect site for your reception—a convenient location, plenty of space, dazzling decorating potential, and a reasonable price. Great! But before you make a commitment and give someone a deposit, ask a few questions and take another look around. Because you are self-catering, you will need to check into a few things a caterer would normally handle.

First and foremost, tell the site representative that you intend to provide the food for your reception and ask about any restrictions on bringing in outside food. Many hotels, convention centers, and other common reception sites require you to use their in-house caterer or the caterers they have exclusive arrangements with for any food you serve in their facility. Other venues recommend a particular caterer; if you don't use that service, the price of renting the facility increases. Community centers, churches, and halls (like VFW or other organizations' halls) tend to be more liberal in their policies regarding outside food than hotels and convention centers. Of course, a private home—if it's large enough for the crowd you're expecting—or even a park can be ideal reception locations, and you can serve anything you'd like.

Once you've got the food issue settled, make another trip through the facility. Assuming you have already evaluated the site's size, parking area, and all-around adequacy for your reception, there are a few additional things you need to take into consideration when you self-cater.

Does the kitchen have a refrigerator and a large table or ample counter space? Although a refrigerator isn't absolutely necessary, it will save you the trouble of dragging in coolers to keep the extras from spoiling before they're served. A counter or table will make replenishing trays and baskets easier and provide a place to store nonperishables until they're needed.

Are there enough electrical outlets and are they located in the area where you plan to set up the serving tables? You won't need many receptacles—just enough for the punch fountain (if you select a reception plan that calls for one) and coffee pot(s). You may also need outlets for a deejay or any decorations (white twinkle lights, for example) you may choose to use.

Will the venue provide any items you would otherwise have to buy or rent, and are they in useable condition? Many facilities have tables, chairs, linens, trash cans, and even some decorations, such as candle holders or floral arrangements, that their customers may use. This can save you some serious money and help you stretch your budget.

Where to Start?

You've got the help and support you'll need from friends and family, and your reception site doesn't care where the food you serve your guests comes from. Now what?

The first two steps—selecting your menu and choosing your helpers—go hand in hand. Each will affect your decision about the other, so consider them together.

Chapters 2 through 7 contain plans for a wide range of receptions. As you decide which plan you want to use, consider your helpers' abilities and the amount of time they can devote to the cause. Also, think about matching your reception's style and mood to your wedding's style and mood. For example, if yours will be a very formal, elegant wedding, you may want to use the Ultimate Reception Plan, while the Basic or Backyard Barbecue Reception will perfectly complement a casual wedding in the park. Be sure to keep your budget in mind as you're deciding on your plan—the fancier the foods, the more you can expect to pay for your reception.

After you've settled on your plan, match your helpers with the job descriptions within your plan. You may want to get their input on which jobs they feel most capable of, but before you ask, narrow down their choices according to what you know of their abilities. For example, if you know your cubicle mate at work couldn't identify a wooden spoon if it whacked her upside the head, don't give her the whole list of jobs to choose from because she might see your reception as a great opportunity to jump into the wonderful world of cooking. Instead, give her the option of making the punch (open a few cans and add ice!) or putting together a fruit tray. Conversely, don't squander the talents of your Pillsbury Bake-Off-winning buddy by asking her to be in charge of the coffee.

As you mull over your list of potential helpers, look for one—preferably the most organized and dependable—to ride herd over your reception committee. He or she doesn't necessarily have to be responsible for preparing a menu item (although they certainly can); this person's job is to coordinate the effort and make sure that the reception preparations run smoothly.

Now, you may be thinking that you don't really need anyone to handle the reception. Don't try to wing it alone! With a reception coordinator, you still maintain control—you decide on the menu and choose your helpers—but you have someone else to handle the details (Green grapes or red? Romaine or iceberg lettuce?) that, piled on top of all the other plans you're stressing about, could send you over the edge.

As you divvy up jobs, write your helpers' names and phone numbers in the appropriate blanks on the job description pages, and fill in the blanks for the date, time, and place of the reception. You'll also find a place to write the number of guests you're expecting to attend the reception—this is not necessarily the same as the number of people you've invited. There is a strange and mysterious formula you can use to calculate how many guests will actually show up: Take the number of people you've invited and multiply by .66. Now, multiply that number by 1.15 and viola! (Example: 300 invited x .66 = 198 x 1.15 = 228 guests.) Who knows why this formula works, but it does.

While it's not an absolute necessity, you may want to get your reception committee together at this point. Introduce your reception coordinator and encourage your team to call her or him with any questions or concerns they may have (assuming this is okay with your coordinator). Hand out photocopies of job descriptions with the blanks filled in and your coordinator's name and phone number written at the top and any diagrams they'll need to each team and give your coordinator photocopies of the entire reception plan. Leave the originals in your book so you'll have a record of who's doing what.

The job descriptions are self-explanatory and very easy to follow, but give your teams a few minutes to look over theirs and ask any questions they may have. If your reception will be held in an unfamiliar location, you may want to provide a map and/or written directions along with the job descriptions.

In addition to bringing your reception helpers together so they can meet each other and get an idea of the big picture, this meeting is a good time to ask for input on the topic of obtaining the food for each team. You'll notice each job description contains a shopping list for the menu item's ingredients. You can handle getting these items in one of three ways. You can ask each team to purchase the items on their individual lists and then reimburse them. Another option is for you or your reception coordinator to go on a massive shopping trip to purchase the items on every shopping list, and then deliver each team's groceries to them. This works well if you want complete control over how much money is spent, you're picky about the brands used, or you only trust your own judgment on the quality of items purchased. The third option is to ask your teams to purchase the items on their lists and suggest that this be their wedding gift to you. Many brides would feel uncomfortable making a request like this, but if you're so inclined and don't think your helpers would be offended by your boldness, go ahead and ask. (If you do this, remember that some of the menu items are far costlier than others. A helper who could afford two cans of coffee may not be able to afford the ingredients for chocolate-dipped strawberries for 200 people.)

That's it! You now have everything in place to put on a spectacular reception and still stay within a reasonable budget. All that's left for you to do is rent, borrow, or buy any dishes, furniture, or equipment your plan calls for (see Chapter 9), order your flowers and wedding and/or groom's cake, keep in touch with your reception coordinator to make sure things are going smoothly, and go shopping for some great gifts for the generous people who are giving you their time to make your self-catered reception a reality.

Chapter 2

The Basic Reception

Simplicity is the key word to describe the Basic Reception. The menu consists of dishes that require no cooking, no special serving equipment, and very little preparation time. While the Basic Reception is short on elbow grease, it can be every bit as elegant and impressive as a reception where nothing but fussy foods with French names are served.

The menu for this plan is fairly light—finger sandwiches, vegetable and fruit trays, cheeseballs, and the like—so it's a good choice for a mid-afternoon reception that falls between lunch and supper. If your wedding and reception will occur around a traditional meal time, you may want to consider more substantial menus such as the ones in the Ultimate or Backyard Barbecue receptions.

Depending on the number of guests you're expecting, you will need eight to 15 reliable friends to help you pull the Basic Reception together. Each person will have to devote five hours or less to the effort, and no one will be so busy they'll have to miss your wedding.

The Menu

Chicken, Tuna, and Ham Salad Finger Sandwiches on
White, Wheat, and Rye Breads
Fresh Fruit Trays with Romanoff Sauce
Pineapple/Dill Cheeseball and Domestic Cheese Tray with
Assorted Crackers
Relish Trays
Fresh Garden Vegetable Trays with Ranch Dressing
Mixed Nuts
Miniature Chocolates
Citrus Fruit Punch

The Helpers

You'll need seven teams—eight to 15 people—to help with this reception. Detailed job descriptions for each team are provided later in this chapter, but here's a quick summary of the type of help for which you're looking.

Setup/Take-Down Team: You'll need two people to set up the hall for the reception and take everything down when it's over. Since this requires some heavy lifting, a buff friend would come in handy on this team. You'll also want to recruit someone with a sense of style to put out tablecloths and floral arrangements and set up the other decorations around the room.

Finger Sandwiches Team: This one's pretty simple. If you have one or two friends who can make sandwiches and open bags of chocolates, you've found your team.

Fruit Trays Team: Another easy assignment for one or two people. Look for helpers who'd be willing to cut up fruit and whip up a batch of dipping sauce.

Cheeseball/Cheese Trays Team: The hardest thing this team of one or two people will have to do is chop nuts and roll cheeseballs in them. They also get to help cut and serve the wedding cake.

Relish Trays Team: If they can open cans and jars, they've got the job! This team of one or two friends also helps cut and serve the groom's cake.

Vegetable Trays Team: Ask one or two friends who don't mind slicing and dicing to fill this job. Absolutely no cooking (or even mixing) skills are required because the dressing served with the vegetables comes from a bottle.

Punch Team: This job requires a bit of brawn—one or two people who can lift buckets of punch and bags of ice without straining something. This team also gets to serve punch to parched partiers during the reception.

The Hardware

In addition to recruiting the people who will help you with your reception, you'll need to rent or purchase the following items. Before whipping out your credit card, however, ask your reception site representative if he or she can provide any of the items free of charge or at a discount. You may also be able to borrow many of the items from friends and family members and save yourself some serious money. See Chapter 9 for complete information on renting or otherwise acquiring the following supplies.

Included in this list are white table linens, centerpieces, floral arrangements, and candelabras. These are staples at traditional wedding receptions, but you may want to use some other type of decorations. Chapter 8 is packed with decorating ideas you may want to consider.

Number of guests:	100	150	200
8' x 30" banquet tables	7	7	7
60" round tables	7	7	7
36" round tables	2	2	2
Folding chairs	100	150	200
90" round white tablecloths	2	2	2
120" round white tablecloths	7	7	7
54" x 120" white tablecloths	7	7	7
21' white skirting sections	7	7	7
3-gallon silver punch bowl and ladle	1	1	1
8" paper or plastic plates	300	450	600
Plastic forks	300	450	600
Floral centerpiece for buffet	1	1	1
Small floral centerpieces	7	7	7
Wedding cake	1	1	1
Groom's cake	1	1	1
Toasting glasses	1 set	1 set	1 set
Cake knife and server	2 sets	2 sets	2 sets
5-branch candelabras	4	4	4
16" taper candles	20	20	20
Guest register & pen	1 set	1 set	1 set

*Note: Have your rentals delivered the day **before** the reception. You don't want your setup team waiting around for a delivery. All items should be there when the team arrives so that they can immediately start setting up.*

Reception Team Job Descriptions

Team 1: Setup/Take-Down Team

Helper #1 _____

Helper #2 _____

Helper #3 _____

Reception Coordinator _____

Reception Location _____

Time of Ceremony _____

Number of Guests _____

Responsibilities

  ❧ Clean out two large plastic trash cans for use at the reception. Since these will be seen by guests, try to find cans that are presentable. Be sure to bring about a half dozen trash can liners.

  ❧ Arrive at the reception site three hours before the ceremony to arrange tables and chairs in their designated locations (see the Basic Reception Room diagram on page 34).

  ❧ Place tablecloths and skirting on tables as follows:
- Seven 8' x 30" tables (wedding cake, gift, punch, and four buffet tables) and 54" x 120" tablecloths. Clip skirting on *before* laying the tablecloth on the table.
- Seven 60" round tables (center buffet and six guest tables) and 120" round tablecloths. No skirting required.
- Two 36" round tables (guest register and groom's cake table) and 90" round tablecloths. No skirting required.

  ❧ If more than one color will be used on the tables, the bride will let you know how the linens should be arranged.

  ❧ The bride will also provide items such as punch bowl, ladle, plates, forks, and centerpieces, and have them delivered to the reception site. Using the diagrams for the Buffet Table, Wedding Cake Table, Punch Table, Groom's Cake Table, and Guest Registry Table (see pages 35 to 37), arrange the items on the appropriate tables.

  ❧ During the reception, help keep the area neat and clean. Keep an eye on the trash cans and replace the liners when needed.

  ❧ At the end of the reception, help with clean up.

Team 2: Finger Sandwiches Team

Helper #1: _____

Helper #2: _____

Reception Coordinator _____

Reception Location _____

Time of Ceremony _____

Number of Guests _____

Responsibilities

❧ Make tuna salad, chicken salad, and ham salad sandwiches according to the recipes on pages 207 and 208 several hours before leaving for the wedding.

❧ Arrive at the reception site one hour before the wedding ceremony and place the sandwich trays, tongs, and miniature chocolates in their designated places using the Buffet Table diagram on page 35. Wrapped chocolates should be placed randomly in their designated places. Help Team 1 with the final touches of setting up the reception site if they need it.

❧ At the end of the reception, help with clean up.

Shopping List

Number of guests:	100	150	200
Sliced white bread	3 loaves	5 loaves	6 loaves
Sliced wheat bread	3 loaves	5 loaves	6 loaves
Sliced rye bread	3 loaves	5 loaves	6 loaves
Store-brand ham salad (12 oz.)*	4	6	8
Store-brand tuna salad (12 oz.)*	4	6	8
Store-brand chicken salad (12 oz.)*	4	6	8
Electric or serrated knife	1	1	1
Small tongs	4	4	4
20" trays (glass or silver)	2	2	2

Recipes for homemade ham, tuna, and chicken salads are given in Chapter 10.

Assorted Finger Sandwiches

Open the loaves of bread and discard the end pieces. Make sandwiches, being sure to spread salad over entire slice of bread. (Use wheat bread for tuna salad, white bread for chicken salad, and rye bread for ham salad.)

Using an electric or serrated knife, cut away the outer crust, leaving a crustless square sandwich.

Cut sandwiches into four equal parts by slicing diagonally to form four triangles.

Place sandwiches on the two trays as shown in the Assorted Finger Sandwiches Tray diagram. Cover sandwiches with a damp paper towel to prevent them from drying out.

Cover the entire tray with plastic wrap and refrigerate.

Assorted Finger Sandwiches Tray

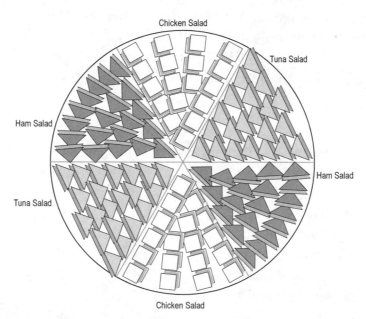

Team 3: Fruit Trays Team

Helper #1 _____

Helper #2 _____

Reception Coordinator _____

Reception Location _____

Time of Ceremony _____

Number of Guests _____

Responsibilities

- Assemble fruit trays (see instructions on page 24) several hours before the wedding.

- Arrive at the reception site one hour before the ceremony and, using the Buffet Table diagram on page 35, place fruit trays and tongs in their designated spot.

- At the end of the reception, help with clean up.

Shopping List

Number of guests:	100	150	200
Fresh green leaf lettuce	6 heads	6 heads	6 heads
Fresh watermelon	1	2	2
Fresh cantaloupe	4	6	8
Fresh honeydew	2	3	4
Fresh strawberries	10 pints	15 pints	20 pints
Sour cream	1 pint	2 pints	3 pints
Light brown sugar	½ lb.	1 lb.	1½ lbs.
Ground cinnamon	1 Tbsp.	2 Tbsp.	3 Tbsp.
20" trays (glass or silver)	2	2	2
Small bowls for fruit sauce	2	2	2
Small tongs	4	4	4
Small spoons for sauce	4	4	4

Fruit Trays

Cantaloupe and honeydew: With a sharp knife, split the melons in half. Using a spoon, scrape out the seeds and soft pulp. Peel the hard, outer rind off with your knife. Cut melon into 1" cubes. Place melon cubes in separate containers, cover with plastic wrap, and refrigerate until you're ready to build your trays.

Strawberries: Gently rinse strawberries under cold running water and shake off excess moisture. *Don't overwash the strawberries or they'll get soggy.* Cut off the white tops along with the stems. Place strawberries in a container, cover with plastic wrap, and refrigerate until you're ready to build your trays.

Watermelon: Split the watermelon in half lengthwise. Split these two pieces widthwise so you have four equal quarters. With your knife, peel away the hard, outer rind. Cut melon into 1" cubes. Place cubes in a container, cover with plastic wrap, and refrigerate until you're ready to build your trays.

Green leaf lettuce: Green leaf lettuce is often confused with iceberg lettuce. When purchasing this at the store, consult with the produce manager to make sure you're buying the correct product. Measure 3" from the core end of the lettuce and cut it off. You'll have about 10 large leaves per head of lettuce. Wash these leaves under cold running water and shake off excess moisture. Place leaves in plastic baggies and refrigerate until you're ready to build your trays.

Romanoff sauce: In a mixing bowl, whip the sour cream, brown sugar, and cinnamon together until well blended. Pour sauce into two small bowls and reserve any remaining sauce for replenishing. Wrap with plastic wrap and refrigerate until you're ready to build your trays.

Putting it all together: Remove the leaf lettuce from the baggies and shake off any excess moisture. Arrange the leaves (shiny side up) fanned out around the outside rim of the trays as shown in the Lettuce Tray diagram on page 25. Overlap the leaves about one inch as you work your way toward the center of the trays. After both trays are completely covered with leaves, place the sauce and fruits in their designated locations as shown in the Fruit Trays diagram on page 25. Cover trays tightly with plastic wrap and refrigerate until ready to serve.

Lettuce Tray (before fruits or vegetables)

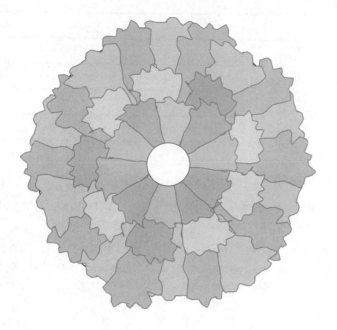

Fruit Tray

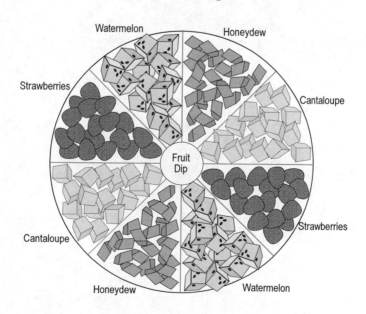

Team 4: Cheeseball/Cheese Trays Team

Helper #1 _____

Helper #2 _____

Reception Coordinator _____

Reception Location _____

Time of Ceremony _____

Number of Guests _____

Responsibilities

- Make the cheeseballs according to the recipe on page 27 early on the day of the wedding or the day before.

- Arrange all cheeses, cheeseballs, and nuts on the trays as illustrated in the Domestic Cheese Tray diagram. Wrap the entire trays with plastic wrap and refrigerate.

Domestic Cheese Tray

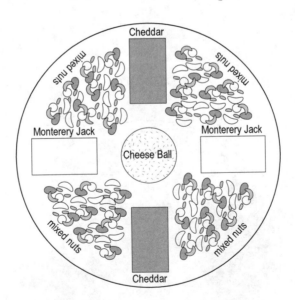

❧ Arrive at the reception site an hour before the ceremony. Using the Buffet Table diagram on page 35, place the trays in their designated locations on the buffet table. Place the spoons on the trays and the knives in the cheese blocks and cheeseball.

❧ Open boxes of crackers and pour them into the baskets; place the baskets in their assigned locations.

❧ Keep an eye on the cracker baskets during the reception and replenish them if needed.

❧ Help cut and serve the wedding cake.

❧ At the end of the reception, help with clean up.

Shopping List

Number of guests:	100	150	200
Sharp cheddar cheese (1½ lb. blocks)	4	4	4
Monterey Jack cheese (1½ lb. blocks)	4	4	4
Cream cheese (8 oz. block)	8	12	16
Crushed pineapple (8 oz. can, drained)	2	3	4
Sharp shredded cheddar (8 oz. pack)	2	3	4
Dill	4 Tbsp.	5 Tbsp.	6 Tbsp.
Chopped pecans (8 oz. bag)	3	4	5
Crackers (1 lb. box)	4	6	8
Mixed nuts (22 oz. can)	6	7	8
20" tray (glass or silver)	2	2	2
Knives for cutting cheese	4	4	4
Spoons for nuts	4	4	4
Cracker basket (white wicker)	2	2	2

Cheeseballs

Remove cream cheese from refrigerator and allow to sit at room temperature for three hours.

In a mixing bowl, combine the cream cheese, shredded cheddar, crushed pineapple, and dill. Mix well.

With your hands, form two equal-sized cheeseballs. Roll the balls in the pecans until thoroughly coated.

Wrap the two pecan-coated cheeseballs in plastic wrap and refrigerate until you're ready to build the trays.

Team 5: Relish Trays Team

Helper #1 _____

Helper #2 _____

Reception Coordinator _____

Reception Location _____

Time of Ceremony _____

Number of Guests _____

Responsibilities

- Assemble relish trays (see instructions on this page).

- Arrive one hour before the ceremony and, using the Buffet Table diagram on page 35, place relish trays in their designated spots on the buffet table.

- Help cut and serve the groom's cake.

- At the end of the reception, help with clean up.

Shopping List

Number of guests:	100	150	200
Gherkin midgets (12 oz. jars)	3	3	4
Kosher dill spears (16 oz. jars)	4	4	5
Green Spanish olives (10 oz. jars)	4	4	5
Ripe olives (5¼ oz. cans)	4	4	4
14" tray (glass or silver)	2	2	2
Small tongs	4	4	4

Relish Trays

This tray may be assembled the day before the reception:

Drain all juices from jars and cans.

Assemble the tray as illustrated in the Assorted Relish Tray diagram on page 29.

Wrap tightly with plastic wrap and refrigerate.

Assorted Relish Tray

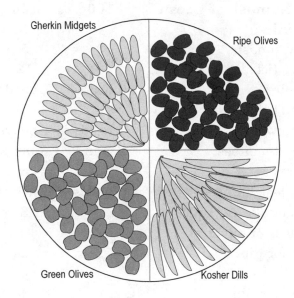

Gherkin Midgets · Ripe Olives · Green Olives · Kosher Dills

Team 6: Vegetable Trays Team

Helper #1 _____

Helper #2 _____

Reception Coordinator _____

Reception Location _____

Time of Ceremony _____

Number of Guests _____

Responsibilities

- Assemble Fresh Vegetable Trays (see instructions on pages 30 and 31).

- Arrive one hour before the ceremony and place vegetable trays and tongs in their spots on the buffet table as shown on the Buffet Table diagram on page 35.

- At the end of the reception, help with clean up.

Shopping List

Number of guests	100	150	200
Fresh zucchini	4	6	8
Fresh yellow squash	3	5	7
Fresh carrot sticks (6 oz. packs)	8	12	16
Fresh broccoli	6 heads	7 heads	8 heads
Fresh celery sticks (6 oz. packs)	8	10	12
Fresh cauliflower	3 heads	4 heads	5 heads
Fresh cherry tomatoes	4 pints	5 pints	6 pints
Fresh cucumbers	6	8	10
Fresh green leaf lettuce	6 heads	6 heads	6 heads
Ranch dressing (24 oz. bottle)	2	3	4
20" trays (glass or silver)	2	2	2
Small bowls for dip	2	2	2
Small tongs 4	4	4	
Small spoons for dip	4	4	4

Vegetable Trays

You can build the vegetable trays the night before the reception. Cover trays with plastic wrap and refrigerate until you're ready to leave for the wedding.

Yellow squash, zucchini, and cucumbers: Wash under cold running water and cut tips off. Split each down the middle lengthwise, then cut widthwise into ¼" slices. Place into separate containers, cover with plastic wrap, and refrigerate until you're ready to build your trays.

Cherry tomatoes: Wash under cold running water and remove any leaves that may be attached. Place into a container and refrigerate until you're ready to build your trays.

Carrot and celery sticks: Remove from package and rinse well with cold running water. Place in separate containers, cover with plastic wrap, and refrigerate until you're ready to build your trays.

Broccoli and cauliflower: Wash under cold running water and cut away large stem. With a pair of sharp scissors, snip off golf ball-size pieces. Place in separate containers, cover with plastic wrap, and refrigerate until you're ready to build your trays.

Green Leaf Lettuce: Green leaf lettuce is often confused with iceberg lettuce. When purchasing this at the store, consult with the produce manager to make sure you're buying the correct product. Measure 3" from the core end of the lettuce and cut it off. You'll have about 10 large leaves per head of lettuce. Wash these leaves under cold running water and shake off excess moisture. Arrange leaves (shiny side up) around the two trays. Fan the leaves out so that they cover the entire tray. The leaves should extend approximately ½" over the rim of the trays.

Putting it all together: Pour the Ranch dressing into the two bowls and place in the center of the leaf-lined tray. Remove vegetables from refrigerator and arrange them as shown in the Fresh Vegetable Tray diagram.

Wrap trays tightly with plastic wrap and refrigerate.

Fresh Vegetable Tray

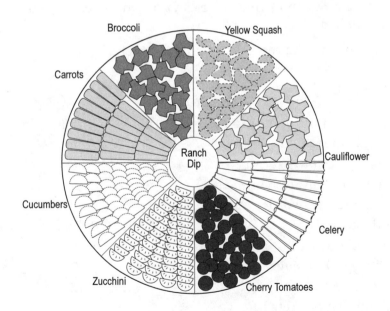

Team 7: Punch Team

Helper #1 _____

Helper #2 _____

Reception Coordinator _____

Reception Location _____

Time of Ceremony _____

Number of Guests _____

Responsibilities

❧ Gather all ingredients for the punch and arrive at the reception site one hour before the wedding. Decide ahead of time where you're going to purchase the ice and pick it up on your way to the reception site. Make the punch at the reception site using the recipe on page 33.

❧ Light the candles on the buffet tables immediately before the reception begins.

❧ Serve the punch during the reception and keep the punch bowl replenished.

❧ At the end of the reception, help with clean up.

Shopping List

Number of guests:	100	150	200
Cranberry juice (64 oz. bottle)	3	5	7
Pineapple juice (46 oz. can)	4	6	8
Orange juice (2 qt. carton)	2	4	6
Ginger ale (2 liter bottle)	4	7	9
Almond extract	4 Tbsp.	6 Tbsp.	8 Tbsp.
Oranges, sliced	3	5	7
Bagged ice (10 lb. bags)	5	7	10
Large ice chest	2	2	3
Clean 5-gallon buckets	2	2	3
Clean 1-gallon buckets	2	2	2
Large spoon (to mix punch)	1	1	1
8 oz. plastic cups	150	200	250
Matches	1 book	1 book	1 book

Citrus Punch

In the 5-gallon buckets, combine cranberry juice, pineapple juice, orange juice, and almond extract (divided equally among the buckets).

Just before the reception, add ginger ale to the mix.

Because the 5-gallon buckets will be too heavy and cumbersome to lift easily, fill the 1-gallon buckets with punch and pour into the punch bowl. (The punch bowl will be waiting for you at the reception site.) Don't fill the bowl to the top—you'll need to add ice. Use the smaller buckets to refill the punch bowl during the reception. Store buckets of punch under the table.

Slice oranges ¼" thick and allow them to float on top of the punch.

Always add the ice directly to the punch bowl, not to the 1- or 5-gallon buckets. Store ice (in an ice chest) under the table.

Introduction to Diagram Section

In this section, you'll find diagrams for setting up your reception hall and the various tables your plan requires. Obviously, a one-size-fits-all approach can't possibly work for every room and every situation, but these diagrams will give you a good place to start in designing your own room setup. You may want to include a bar, a band, and a dance floor in your reception. Or perhaps you'd like to provide more dining tables for your guests or eliminate the groom's cake table. Feel free to modify the room to fit your needs, your taste, and your budget.

Basic Reception

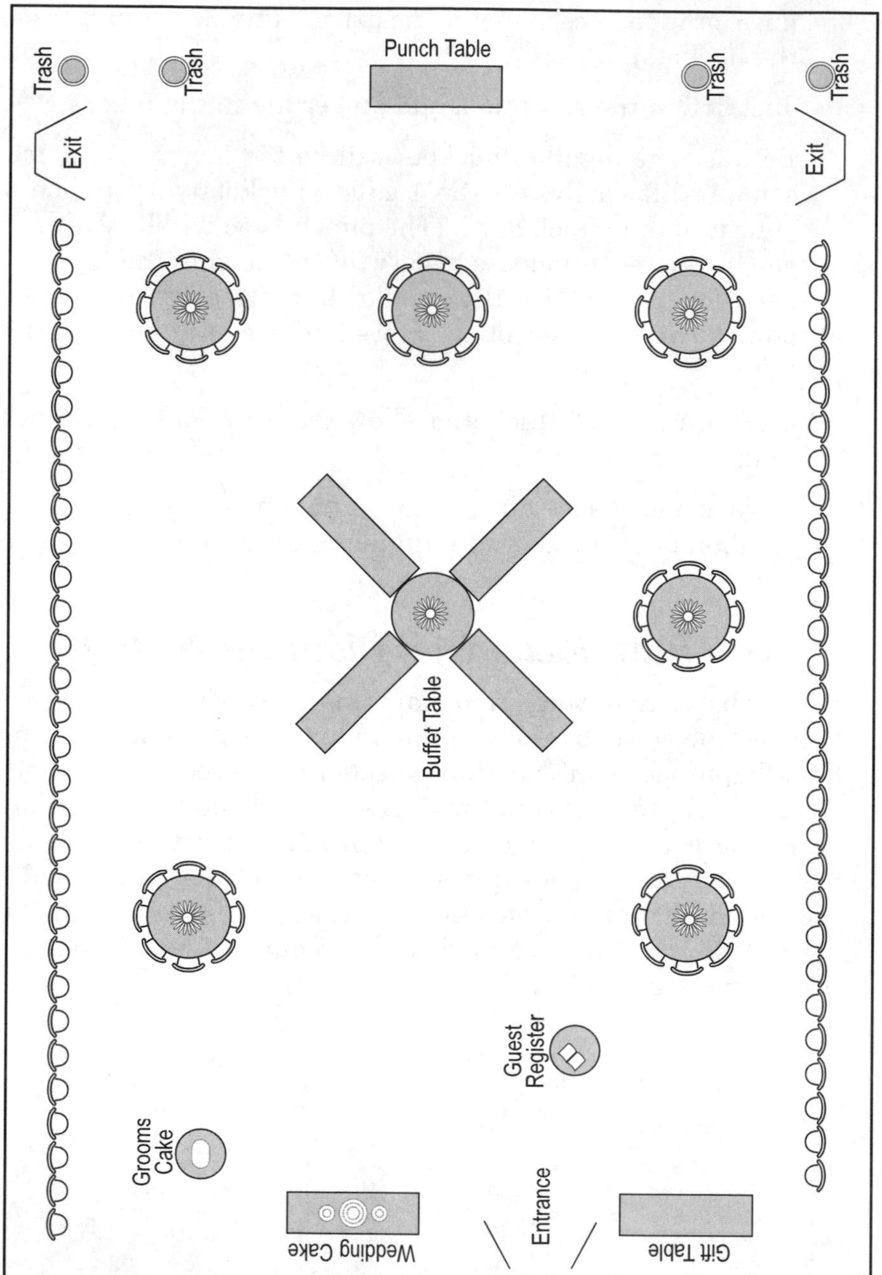

Punch Table

Trash

Trash

Trash

Trash

Exit

Exit

Buffet Table

Grooms Cake

Wedding Cake

Guest Register

Entrance

Gift Table

Buffet Table for
Basic Reception

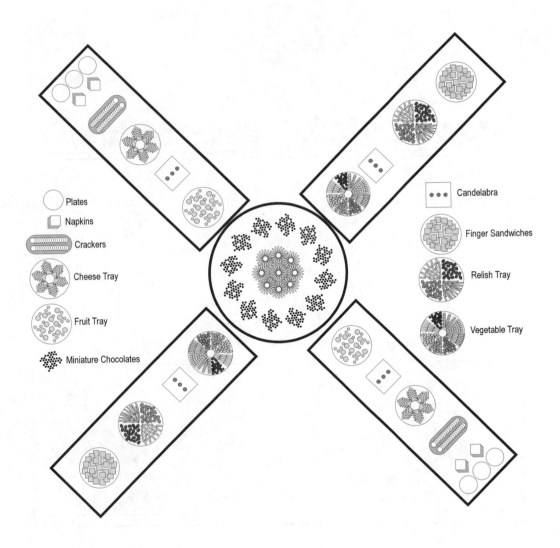

Plates

Napkins

Crackers

Cheese Tray

Fruit Tray

Miniature Chocolates

Candelabra

Finger Sandwiches

Relish Tray

Vegetable Tray

Basic Wedding Cake Table

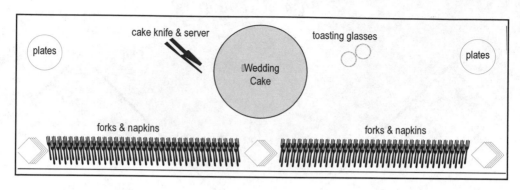

Basic Punch Table

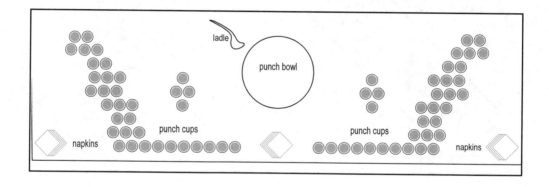

Basic Groom's Cake Table

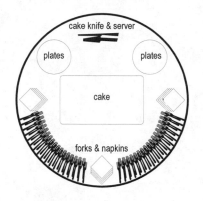

Basic Guest Registry Table

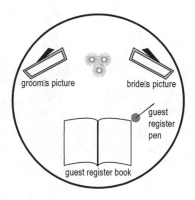

 *Chapter 3*

The Ultimate Reception

If you want to dazzle your guests, this is the plan for you! The Ultimate Reception takes a bit more work than most of the other plans in this book, but because the results are spectacular, it's well worth it.

This plan is the perfect choice if your reception will take place at lunch or supper time. Your guests will have plenty of main-dish choices to fill up on—Lush and Lavish Meatballs, Chicken Salad Pastry Swans, and Shrimp and Crabmeat Delights—along with marinated vegetables, cheese trays, and wedding cookies to fill in the holes. And the Chocolate-Dipped Strawberry Trees will awe them with the extravagant lengths you and your reception team went to for them (you don't have to tell them how easy it was to do).

You'll need 12 to 20 reliable friends to help you pull together the Ultimate Reception, depending on the number of guests you're inviting. Except for the Setup/Take-Down Team, no one will have to do a lot of work right before your wedding because most of the food can be prepared one or two days ahead of time. All your helpers will have to do on your wedding day is put the final touches on their dishes and sob uncontrollably as you walk down the aisle.

The Menu
Shrimp and Crabmeat Delights
Chicken Salad Pastry Swans
Lush and Lavish Meatballs
Chocolate-Dipped Strawberry Trees
Domestic Cheese Trays with Assorted Crackers
Marinated Vegetables
Mixed Nuts
Butterfly Wedding Cookies
Freshly Brewed Regular and Decaffeinated Coffee
Citrus Fruit Punch

The Helpers

You'll need 10 teams—12 to 20 people—to help with this reception. Detailed job descriptions for each team are provided later in this chapter, but here's a quick summary of the type of help you're looking for.

Setup/Take-Down Team: Your friends who spend all their free time in a gym would be perfect for this team of two or three people because it requires some heavy lifting. At least one person on the team should have a bit of an artistic flair so they can lay out the tablecloths and centerpieces and make everything pretty.

Shrimp and Crabmeat Delights Team: No cooking—just coring, chopping, mixing, and stuffing—is required of the one or two people on this team. You might want to look for a married couple or two roommates for this job; they live in the same household and share a kitchen so they won't have to worry about transporting cooking utensils and supplies.

Chicken Salad Pastry Swans Team: Save this one for two of your pals who really like to cook. Although the recipe's not too tough, this team will need to know their way around a kitchen and devote about three to five hours to the cause. The swan bodies require a lot of refrigerator space, so you might want to recruit people from two different households so they'll have a couple of refrigerators between them.

Lush and Lavish Meatballs Team: Here's another job for one person, a married couple, or roommates. The meatballs can be made weeks in advance and frozen, and the sauce is a snap to put together on the big day.

Chocolate-Dipped Strawberry Trees: This team's job description is the longest of the bunch, but theirs isn't an especially difficult job. Ask a couple of detail-oriented people with an artistic flair to handle this one.

Cheeseball/Cheese Trays Team: The hardest thing this team of one or two people will have to do is chop nuts and roll cheeseballs in them. They also get to help cut and serve the wedding cake.

Marinated Vegetables Team: Here's a pretty simple job for one or two people. If they can turn on a stove, open a few cans, and chop veggies, they can handle this job. They also get the honor of cutting and serving the groom's cake.

Wedding Cookies and Leather Leaf Team: Actually, this doesn't even have to be a team; your best baking buddy can handle this one alone. This person will also open a few cans of nuts and line the serving tables with leather leaf. It's a piece of cake.

Coffee Team: This is another job for one or two people. There's very little advance preparation and no culinary prowess required to handle the coffee-making duties during the reception.

Punch Team: This job requires a bit of brawn—one or two people who can lift buckets of punch and bags of ice without straining something. The punch recipe is simple, so you don't have to recruit a master chef.

The Hardware

In addition to recruiting the people who will help you with your reception, you'll need to rent or purchase the items listed on page 42. Before whipping out your credit card, however, ask your reception site representative if he or she can provide any of the items free of charge or at a discount. You may also be able to borrow many of the items from friends and family members and save yourself some serious money. See Chapter 9 for complete information on renting or otherwise acquiring these supplies.

Included in this list are white table linens, centerpieces, floral arrangements, and candelabras. These are staples at traditional wedding receptions, but you may want to use some other type of decorations. Chapter 8 is packed with decorating ideas you may want to consider.

Number of guests:	100	150	200
60" round tables	7	7	7
8' x 30" banquet tables	8	8	8
36" round tables	4	4	4
Folding chairs	100	150	200
120" round white tablecloths	7	7	7
90" round white tablecloths	4	4	4
54" x 120" white tablecloths	8	8	8
21' white skirting segments	8	8	8
5-gallon punch fountain	1	1	1
5-oz. glass punch cups	125	175	225
90-cup stainless steel coffee urns	2	2	2
Coffee cups	75	100	125
Coffee saucers	75	100	125
Sugar bowls	4	4	4
Creamers	2	2	2
Spoons	75	100	125
Forks	275	400	550
8" glass plates	275	400	550
5-branch candelabras	6	6	6
16" white tapered candles	30	30	30
Floral centerpiece for buffet	1	1	1
Floral centerpieces for guest tables	7	7	7
Floral centerpiece for coffee table	1	1	1
Floral centerpiece for guest registry table	1	1	1
18"h x 11"w white columns *(from a craft store or garden center)*	5	5	5
Wedding cake	1	1	1
Groom's cake	1	1	1
Cake knife and server	2 Sets	2 Sets	2 Sets
Engraved napkins	425	625	725
Guest book and pen	1 set	1 set	1 set
Toasting glasses	1 set	1 set	1 set

*Note: Have your rentals delivered the day **before** the reception. You don't want your setup team waiting around for a delivery. All items should be there when the team arrives so that they can immediately start setting up.*

Reception Team Job Descriptions

Team 1: Setup/Take-Down Team

Helper #1 _____

Helper #2 _____

Helper #3 _____

Reception Coordinator _____

Reception Location _____

Time of Ceremony _____

Number of Guests _____

Responsibilities

❧ Clean out two large plastic trash cans for use at the reception. Because these will be seen by guests, try to find cans that are presentable. Be sure to bring about a half dozen trash can liners.

❧ Arrive at the reception site about four hours before the ceremony to arrange tables and chairs in their designated locations (see the Ultimate Reception Room diagram on page 63).

❧ Place tablecloths and skirting on tables as follows:
  - Eight 8' x 30" tables (wedding cake, gift, punch, and four buffet tables) and 54" x 120" tablecloths. Clip skirting on *before* laying the tablecloth on the table.
  - Seven 60" round tables (center buffet and six guest tables) and 120" round tablecloths. No skirting required.
  - Four 36" round tables (guest registry, groom's cake, and two soiled dish tables) and 90" round tablecloths. No skirting.

❧ If more than one color will be used on the tables, the bride will let you know how the linens should be arranged.

❧ The bride will provide items such as dishes, silverware, the punch fountain, chafing dishes, and centerpieces and have them delivered to the reception site. Using the diagrams for the Buffet Table, Wedding Cake Table, Punch Table, Coffee Table, Groom's Cake Table, and Guest Registry Table (see pages 64 to 66), arrange the items on the appropriate tables.

❧ During the reception, help keep the area neat and clean. Keep an eye on the trash cans and replace the liners when they're full.

❧ At the end of the reception, help with clean up and return all rented items to the location of the room where they were delivered.

Team 2: Shrimp and Crabmeat Delights Team

Helper #1: _____

Helper #2: _____

Reception Coordinator _____

Reception Location _____

Time of Ceremony _____

Number of Guests _____

Responsibilities

❧ The day before the reception, make Shrimp and Crabmeat Delights according to the recipes on pages 44 and 45. Because these need to be refrigerated, you might want to clean out your fridge ahead of time so you'll have plenty of room to store them.

❧ Arrive at the reception site no more than an hour before the ceremony and place the trays of Shrimp and Crabmeat Delights on the buffet tables as shown on the Buffet Table diagram on page 64. Your extra Delights should be refrigerated at the reception site. If no refrigerator is available, store them in a shady, cool spot out of direct sunlight.

❧ Keep an eye on your trays during the reception and replenish them when needed.

❧ At the end of the reception, help with clean up.

Shopping List

Number of guests	100	150	200
For Shrimp and Crabmeat Delights			
Fresh Roma tomatoes	75	100	125
Baby corn (15 oz. can, drained)	4	6	8
Sliced black olives (3.8 oz., drained)	1	2	3
Sliced pimientos (7 oz. jar, drained)	1	2	2
Seafood Salad Stuffing (recipe given)	7 lbs.	11 lbs.	14 lbs.

Number of guests	100	150	200
For Seafood Salad Stuffing			
Mayonnaise	2 cups	3 cups	4 cups
Sour cream	1 cup	1½ cups	2 cups
Salt	2 tsp.	3 tsp.	4 tsp.
White ground pepper	1 tsp.	2 tsp.	3 tsp.
Melted butter (warm, not hot)	12 oz.	18 oz.	24 oz.
Frozen bay shrimp (thaw/drain)	1½ lbs.	2¼ lbs.	3 lbs.
Frozen imitation crab (thaw/drain)	2½ lbs.	3¾ lbs.	5 lbs.
Fresh celery, diced	4 cups	6 cups	8 cups
Fresh green onion, chopped	2 cups	3 cups	4 cups
Dried parsley, ½ oz. jar	1	2	3
20" round tray (glass or silver)	2	2	2
Small tongs	4	4	4

Shrimp and Crabmeat Delights

Remove the small core from the tomatoes. Slice the tomatoes in half lengthwise. With a spoon, scrape out the seeds and the soft inner contents of the tomato halves.

Stuff the tomato halves with the Seafood Salad Stuffing (recipe following on this page).

Slice the baby corn in half lengthwise. Place a corn half on top of each stuffed tomato. Place a sliced olive on top of the corn and lay a strip of pimento across the olive. Sprinkle with chopped parsley

Arrange Delights on trays and loosely cover with plastic wrap and refrigerate. If you have any extras, put them on cookie sheets and take them with you to replenish the trays during the reception.

Seafood Salad Stuffing

Whip mayonnaise, sour cream, salt, and pepper together in a large mixing bowl. Slowly whip butter into the mayonnaise mixture.

Using a rubber spatula, fold in the shrimp, crab, celery, and onion. Gently toss until well blended. Be careful not to overmix.

Cover tightly with plastic wrap and refrigerate until ready to stuff tomatoes.

Team 3: Chicken Salad Pastry Swans Team

Helper #1 _____

Helper #2 _____

Reception Coordinator _____

Reception Location _____

Time of Ceremony _____

Number of Guests _____

Responsibilities

  ❧ The day before the reception, make the pastry and chicken salad for the Chicken Salad Pastry Swans according to the recipes on pages 47 and 48. Assemble and stuff the swans a few hours before the reception. Because the swans need to be refrigerated, you might want to clean out your fridge ahead of time so you'll have plenty of room to store them.

  ❧ Arrive at the reception site no more than an hour before the ceremony and place the trays of Swans on the buffet tables as shown on the Buffet Table diagram on page 64. Your extra Swans should be refrigerated at the reception site. If no refrigerator is available, store them in a shady, cool spot out of direct sunlight.

  ❧ Keep an eye on your trays during the reception and replenish them when needed.

  ❧ At the end of the reception, help with clean up.

Shopping List

Number of guests:	100	150	200
For Swan Pastry			
Water	4 qts.	6 qts.	8 qts.
Margarine	4 lbs.	6 lbs.	8 lbs.
Bread flour, sifted	12 cups	18 cups	24 cups
Eggs, large	6 doz.	9 doz.	12 doz.
Pastry bags	1–2	1–2	1–2
20" round trays (silver or glass)	4	4	4

Number of guests:	100	150	200
For Chicken Salad			
Mayonnaise	5 pints	7½ pints	10 pints
Sweet pickle relish	2 cups	3 cups	4 cups
Salt	2 Tbsp.	3 Tbsp.	4 Tbsp.
White pepper	2 tsp.	3 tsp.	4 tsp.
Tarragon vinegar	1 Tbsp.	1½ Tbsp.	2 Tbsp.
Worcestershire sauce	2 Tbsp.	3 Tbsp.	4 Tbsp.
Cooked white chicken meat,diced	10 lbs.	15 lbs.	20 lbs.
Hard-boiled eggs, chopped	8	12	16
Finely chopped green onion	2 cups	3 cups	4 cups
Finely chopped celery	4 cups	6 cups	8 cups

Chicken Salad Pastry Swans (Pastry Dough)

Note: This recipe makes 25 swans—home ovens are too small to bake more than 25 at a time. For 100 guests, make four batches. For 150 guests, make six batches. For 200 guests, make eight batches. The swan necks and bodies may be made the day before the reception and do not need to be refrigerated. Stuff and assemble them with chicken salad a few hours before the wedding.

Recipe for one batch of Pastry Swans

1 qt.water
3 cups bread flour, sifted

1 lb.margarine
18 large eggs

Combine margarine and water and bring to a rolling boil. While whipping constantly with a wire whip or electric mixer, add three cups of flour and cook until mixture rolls free from the sides of the pot (about one minute).

Still whipping constantly, slowly add 18 eggs until mixture reaches a medium stiffness (about two minutes). Remove from heat and allow to cool for 10 minutes.

Without inserting a pastry tip, load your pastry bag half full with dough. Pipe out 25 lemon-sized dough balls spaced 2" apart on ungreased cookie sheets, keeping the sizes consistent. These are the swan bodies. You won't use all of the dough in this step, so leave the remainder in the bowl.

Bake dough balls at 375 degrees until they become dark golden brown (about 30 to 35 minutes). Remove pastry balls from the oven and allow to cool for 30 minutes. (If pastries begin to fall while cooling, immediately place them back in the oven to bake a little longer. They should recover just fine.)

Squeeze any remaining dough from the pastry bag back into the bowl with the leftover dough. You are now ready to begin the construction of the necks.

Without cleaning the pastry bag, insert a standard round pastry tip. This tip should have a round opening about the size of a pencil eraser.

Load the pastry bag with the remaining dough. Pipe out neck forms in the shape of a question mark (?). Practice piping out a few of these to be sure the size of the neck is in proportion to the body of the swan.

Place necks in oven at 375 degrees for 12 to 14 minutes until they become dark golden brown. Remove from oven and allow to cool 30 minutes.

Cut the body in half to create a top and bottom. Cut the top part in half to create the wings. Stuff chicken salad mixture in the bottom half and place the two wings on top. Insert the neck into the chicken salad between the wings.

Chicken Salad

To make dressing, combine mayonnaise, pickle relish, salt, pepper, vinegar, and Worcestershire sauce in a large mixing bowl. Using a wire whip, blend all ingredients well. Set aside.

Place diced chicken, chopped eggs, chopped green onions, and celery in a large mixing bowl. Pour dressing mixture over the chicken mixture. Blend all ingredients well using a rubber spatula. Be careful not to overmix.

Cover tightly with plastic wrap and refrigerate until you're ready to assemble the swans. Once the swans are assembled, they must be refrigerated.

Team 5: Lush and Lavish Meatballs Team

Helper #1 _____

Helper #2 _____

Reception Coordinator _____

Reception Location _____

Time of Ceremony _____

Number of Guests _____

Responsibilities

❧ Make Lush and Lavish Meatballs according to the recipe on pages 49 and 50. The meatballs can be made a few weeks before the wedding and frozen; you might want to clean out your freezer ahead of time so you'll have plenty of room to store them.

❧ Arrive at the reception site with the hot meatballs no more than an hour before the ceremony. Using the Chafing Dish Assembly Instructions (Chapter 9), set up the chafing dishes as shown on the Buffet Table diagram on page 64. (You don't have to provide the chafing dishes—they'll be waiting for you at the reception hall.) Light the Sternos and pour the meatballs in the pans; cover with the lids.

❧ At the end of the reception, help with clean up.

Shopping List

Number of guests:	100	150	200
For Meatballs			
White bread, crusts removed	18 slices	24 slices	30 slices
Lean ground beef	12 lbs.	16 lbs.	20 lbs.
Fresh, large eggs, beaten	6	8	10
Onion, diced fine	3 cups	4 cups	5 cups
Beef broth, canned	3 cups	4 cups	5 cups
Garlic cloves, diced fine	6	8	10
Salt	2 Tbsp.	3 Tbsp.	4 Tbsp.
Paprika	2 Tbsp.	3 Tbsp.	4 Tbsp.
Ground black pepper	1 Tbsp.	1½ Tbsp.	2 Tbsp.
Thyme, dried	2 Tbsp.	3 Tbsp.	4 Tbsp.
Yield	225	335	450

Number of guests:	100	150	200
For Sauce			
Chili sauce, 12 oz. bottle	6	8	10
Grape jelly, 1 lb. jar	3	4	5
Sterno, 8 oz. cans	4	4	4
Matches	1 book	1 book	1 book
Serving spoons	4	4	4

Lush and Lavish Meatballs

Note: These meatballs may be made several weeks in advance and frozen.

Preheat oven to 350 degrees.

In a large mixing bowl, soak bread in cold water for two minutes. Drain and squeeze out excess moisture.

Add ground beef, eggs, onion, broth, garlic, salt, paprika, pepper, and thyme and mix well.

Shape into 1" balls, place on cookie sheets, and bake for 12 to 15 minutes.

Remove meatballs from oven and allow to cool for one hour. Place in zipper baggies and freeze. Take the meatballs out of the freezer to thaw in the refrigerator the day prior to the wedding.

Early on the day of the wedding, divide thawed meatballs among several high-lipped pans that will fit in your oven.

Make Lush and Lavish Sauce (recipe follows).

Pour hot sauce over cooked meatballs. Gently toss the meatballs to coat them entirely with sauce. Bake in 350 degree oven until bubbly hot, about 30 minutes.

Remove from oven. Wrap tightly with foil and take to the reception site.

Lush and Lavish Sauce

Combine chili sauce and grape jelly in a large mixing bowl. Using a wire whip, blend mixture until smooth.

Place mixture in a large saucepan and cook until hot.

Team 5: Chocolate-Dipped Strawberry Trees Team

Helper #1 ______________________________

Helper #2 ______________________________

Reception Coordinator ______________________________

Reception Location ______________________________

Time of Ceremony ______________________________

Number of Guests ______________________________

Responsibilities

- Make the tree forms several days ahead of time. Dip the strawberries and assemble the trees the day before the reception (recipe and instructions on pages 51 to 53). The trees need to be refrigerated; clean out your refrigerator ahead of time so you'll have plenty of room to store them.
- Arrive at the reception hall no more than one hour before the ceremony. Place the trees in their designated places on the buffet table using the Buffet Table diagram on page 64 to guide you.
- Help with clean up after the reception is over.

Shopping List

Number of guests:	**100**	**150**	**200**
Green leaf lettuce	4 heads	4 heads	4 heads
Strawberries	30 pints	36 pints	42 pints
Semisweet chocolate chips, 12 oz. pkg	7	10	14
White Styrofoam cones 18" h x 5" diameter base	2	2	2
White Styrofoam circles, 12" diameter x 1" thick	2	2	2
Toothpicks	350	350	350
Glue	1 bottle	1 bottle	1 bottle
20" round trays (silver or glass)	2	2	2
Small tongs	4	4	4

Strawberry Trees

Building the Form

Turn cones upside down and apply a generous amount of glue to the bases.

Center the cone bases in the middle of the Styrofoam circles. Press cones down firmly to the circles to ensure that the glue adheres.

Place the finished Styrofoam tree forms in a safe place and allow to dry for 48 hours.

After trees are completely dried, insert the toothpicks into the cones at a 45-degree angle (pointing up) and approximately 1" apart. Each cone should hold about 175 toothpicks. When the tree is standing upright, the toothpicks should all be aimed upward.

Chocolate-Dipped Strawberries

Place chocolate in a large stainless steel bowl. Using a double-boiler, lower the bowl into a pot of boiling water to melt the chocolate. Stir occasionally until chocolate is creamy and smooth.

Hold a strawberry by its leaves and dip into the melted chocolate, submerging the strawberry completely. Gently shake off dripping chocolate.

Place the coated strawberry directly on an ungreased cookie sheet. Continue dipping until all berries are coated and placed on cookie sheets. Refrigerate the chocolate strawberries for one hour until chocolate is completely hardened.

Place strawberries in zipper bags and refrigerate again until you're ready to build the trees.

Assembling the Trees

Green leaf lettuce is often confused with iceberg lettuce. When purchasing this at the store, consult with the produce manager to make sure you're buying the correct product. Measure 3" from the core end of the lettuce and cut it off. You'll have about 10 large leaves per head of lettuce. Rinse and shake off excess moisture.

Starting at the base of the Styrofoam cones, press the leaves (shiny side out) through the toothpicks onto the cones. Continue this process until the entire cone is covered with lettuce. Fan the remaining leaves around the base of the cone to cover the Styrofoam circle.

Starting at the base of the cone, press a strawberry into each toothpick with the strawberry's point aimed outward. Continue this process around the base and work your way up the tree one level at a time until entire tree is completely covered.

Place both trees into your refrigerator until you're ready to leave for the wedding. You may have to remove one or two refrigerator shelves to have enough space for both trees.

When you're ready to leave for the reception hall, take the two finished trees, your trays, and the bagged chocolate strawberries. Drive carefully and avoid any sudden stops or abrupt turns.

Place the trays in their designated locations on the buffet table (see the Buffet Table diagram on page 64). Set the two trees in the center of the trays.

Arrange the chocolate strawberries on the trays at the base of the cone and continue outward to the edge of the tray. Don't be afraid to stack the chocolate berries, if necessary.

Place two tongs next to each tree.

Team 6: Cheeseball/Cheese Trays Team

Helper #1 _____

Helper #2 _____

Reception Coordinator _____

Reception Location _____

Time of Ceremony _____

Number of Guests _____

Responsibilities

- Make the cheeseballs the day before (see the recipe on page 55).

- Arrive at the reception hall an hour before the wedding and assemble the cheese trays (see assembly instructions on page 55).

- Keep an eye on your trays and cracker baskets and replenish them if necessary.

- Help cut and serve the wedding cake.

- At the end of the reception, help with clean up.

Shopping List

Number of guests:	100	150	200
Sharp cheddar cheese (1½ lb. blocks)	4	4	4
Monterey Jack cheese (1½ lb. blocks)	4	4	4
Cream cheese (8 oz. block)	8	12	16
Crushed pineapple, drained (8 oz. can)	2	3	4
Sharp shredded cheddar (8 oz. pack)	2	3	4
Dill	4 Tbsp.	5 Tbsp.	6 Tbsp.
Chopped pecans (8 oz. bag)	3	4	5
Red seedless grapes, bunches	4	4	4
Limes	3	3	3
Strawberries	1 pt	1pt	1 pt
Crackers (2 lb. box)	2	3	4
20" tray (glass or silver)	2	2	2
Cake stands	2	2	2
Knives	8	8	8
Cracker basket	2	2	2

Cheeseballs

Remove cream cheese from the refrigerator and allow to sit at room temperature for three hours.

In a mixing bowl, combine the cream cheese, shredded cheddar, crushed pineapple, and dill. Mix well.

With your hands, form two equal-sized cheeseballs. Roll the balls in pecans until thoroughly coated. Wrap the two pecan-coated cheeseballs in plastic wrap and refrigerate until you're ready to build the trays.

Green leaf lettuce is often confused with iceberg lettuce. When purchasing this at the store, consult with the produce manager to make sure you're buying the correct product. Measure 3" from the core end of the lettuce and cut it off. You'll have about 10 large leaves per head of lettuce. Wash the leaves under cold water, shake dry, and place in a plastic bag.

Cut lemons and limes into eight wedges each and place in a plastic bag.

Assembling the Trays at the Reception Site

Using the Buffet Table diagram on page 64, place the two trays and the wicker baskets in their spots on the buffet table. Place a cake stand in the middle of each tray.

Remove the leaf lettuce from the plastic bags. Fan out the lettuce leaves (shiny side up) around the entire top surface of the cake stand. The lettuce should extend no further than ¼" outside the edge of the cake stand (see the Lettuce Tray diagram on page 56).

Place the cheeseballs in the center of the cake stands (see the Cheese Trays diagram on page 56). With a pair of scissors, take the grapes and clip out small clumps and arrange them around the cheeseball.

Randomly place the strawberries and lemon and lime wedges among the clumps of grapes.

Place the blocks of cheese on the tray surface, with two blocks cheddar and two blocks Monterey Jack per tray. Insert two cheese knives into each cheeseball and place two knives on the side of each tray.

Tray with Lettuce

Ultimate Cheese Tray

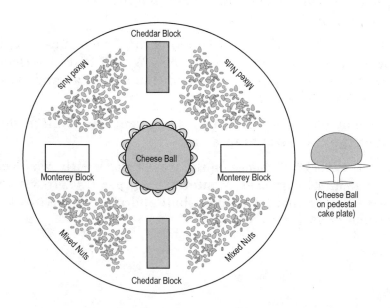

Team 7: Marinated Vegetables Team

Helper #1 _____

Helper #2 _____

Reception Coordinator _____

Reception Location _____

Time of Ceremony _____

Number of Guests _____

Responsibilities

❧ Make Marinated Vegetables (see recipe on page 58) 24 to 48 hours before the reception.

❧ Arrive one hour before the ceremony and place vegetables and serving spoons in their designated places on the buffet table (see Buffet Table diagram on page 64).

❧ Help cut and serve the groom's cake.

❧ At the end of the reception, help with clean up.

Shopping List

Number of guests:	100	150	200
Sugar	5 cups	7½ cups	10 cups
White vinegar	3¾ cups	5¾ cups	7½ cups
Tarragon vinegar	2 Tbsp.	3 Tbsp.	4 Tbsp.
Vegetable oil	2½ cups	3¾ cups	5 cups
Black pepper	5 tsp.	2 Tbsp.	3 Tbsp.
Salt	1 Tbsp.	1½ Tbsp.	2 Tbsp.
French-style green beans, (16 oz can, drained)	5	8	10
Green peas (16 oz can, drained)	5	8	10
Shoepeg corn (16 oz can, drained)	5	8	10
Diced pimientos (2 oz jar, drained)	5	8	10
Celery, diced	5 cups	8 cups	10 cups
Green pepper, diced	5	8	10
Green onion, diced, bunches	5	8	10
20" round trays (glass or silver)	2	2	2
Serving spoons	4	4	4

Marinated Vegetables

To make marinade, combine sugar, vinegars, oil, pepper, and salt in a saucepan and cook over medium heat until sugar is dissolved. Refrigerate for two hours.

Combine vegetables in a large mixing bowl and add the marinade. Mix well, cover, and refrigerate until ready to serve. Stir occasionally.

Transfer the vegetables to trays at the reception site.

Team 8: Butterfly Wedding Cookies and Leather Leaf Team

Helper #1 _____

Reception Coordinator _____

Reception Location _____

Time of Ceremony _____

Number of Guests _____

Responsibilities

- Make Butterfly Wedding Cookies (see page 59) the day before the reception.

- Make sure you have the leather leaf the day before the wedding. Without removing the rubber bands that will be wrapped around the bunches of leather leaf when you get it from the florist, rinse the bunches with cold water, place in a trash bag, and refrigerate.

- When preparing to leave for the reception, remove the leather leaf from the trash bag. Cut off the leafless stems. Place the leaves back into the trash bag and take to the reception site.

- Arrive at the reception site an hour before the ceremony. Following the Leather Leaf Placement diagram on page 64, place leather leaf (shiny side up) around the buffet table.

- Using the Buffet Table diagram on page 64, place the cookies on the buffet table in their assigned spot.

- Pour mixed nuts into bowls, insert two spoons in each bowl, and place them in their designated spots on the buffet table.

- At the end of the reception, help with clean up.

Shopping List

Number of guests:	100	150	200
Butter, softened	4 cups	6 cups	8 cups
Vanilla extract	1 Tbsp.	1½ Tbsp.	2 Tbsp.
Flour, all purpose	6 cups	9 cups	12 cups
Powdered sugar, sifted	3 cups	4½ cups	6 cups
Cornstarch 1 cup	1½ cups	2 cups	
Gourmet jelly beans, small*	2 cups	3 cups	4 cups
Coconut, flaked	2½ cups	3¾ cups	5 cups
Leather leaf, bunches	6	6	6
Mixed nuts, 16 oz can	4	6	8
Glass bowls, (cantaloupe size)	4	4	4
Small serving spoons	8	8	8

* Use gourmet jelly beans only—regular jelly beans will melt during baking.

Butterfly Wedding Cookies

Using an electric mixer, beat the butter and vanilla at medium speed until creamy.

Combine flour, sugar, and cornstarch in a large bowl and slowly add to the butter mixture; blend well. Cover and refrigerate for two hours to allow the dough to firm up.

Shape into 1" balls. Roll the ball between your hands to form a small log. Roll the dough logs into the coconut.

Place on ungreased cookie sheet about 1" apart. Pinch the middle of the logs with your thumb and middle finger to form a bowtie.

Place the gourmet jelly bean in the center of each bowtie to form the butterfly's body.

Bake at 300 degrees for 25 minutes or until coconut is golden brown.

Allow to cool and place gently in plastic bags.

Team 9: Coffee Team

Helper #1 _____

Helper #2 _____

Reception Coordinator _____

Reception Location _____

Time of Ceremony _____

Number of Guests _____

Responsibilities

❧ Make small placards or signs for regular and decaffeinated coffee. You may want to make these on your computer or write them by hand in calligraphy.

❧ The coffee will take 30 minutes to an hour to brew. Arrive at the reception site in plenty of time for the coffee to be ready by the beginning of the reception. The coffee urns will be waiting for you at the reception site.

❧ Using the Coffee Table diagram on page 65, place the small bowls and creamers in their assigned spots. Fill half the bowls with sugar and the other half with sweetener packets. Fill the creamers with half-and-half. Place the coffee signs/placards in front of the appropriate coffee urn. Place back-up supplies under the table.

❧ During the reception, keep an eye on the coffee table and replenish sugar, cream, and so forth as necesary.

❧ At the end of the reception, help with clean up.

Shopping List

Number of guests:	100	150	200
Regular coffee	10 oz.	15 oz.	20 oz.
Decaffeinated coffee	10 oz.	15 oz.	20 oz.
Water per urn	50 cups	75 cups	90 cups
Sugar	1 lb.	1½ lbs.	2 lbs.
Sweet 'N Low (Packets)	50	75	100
Equal (Packets)	25	35	50
Cream (half-and-half)	2 qts.	3 qts.	4 qts.
Glass bowls (softball size)	6	6	6
Regular sign, Decaffeinated sign	1 ea.	1 ea.	1 ea.
12' three-pronged extension cords	2	2	2

Coffee

At the reception site, make sure that the coffee table is located near electrical outlets. You may have to move the table closer to an outlet if you don't have easy access. Use your extension cords if necessary.

Remove the lids, filters, and stems from the coffee pots. Fill the pots to the correct water line (look for lines inside the pots). Reinsert the stems and filters. Fill the filters with the desired amount of coffee (read the labels on the coffee can to find out how much coffee to measure into the filters). Secure the lids and turn the coffee urns on. The coffee will take from 30 minutes to an hour to brew.

Team 10: Punch Team

Helper #1 _____

Helper #2 _____

Reception Coordinator _____

Reception Location _____

Time of Ceremony _____

Number of Guests _____

Responsibilities

❧ Gather all ingredients for the punch and arrive at the reception site one hour before the wedding. Decide ahead of time where you're going to get the ice and pick it up on your way to the reception site. Make the punch at the reception site according to the recipe on page 62.

❧ Fill the punch fountain with punch and keep it replenished during the reception. The fountain will be waiting for you at the hall, but you'll need to bring an extension cord (see Shopping List) in case the fountain's cord won't easily reach an outlet.

❧ Light all candles on the buffet table right before the reception begins.

❧ At the end of the reception, help with clean up.

Shopping List

Number of guests:	100	150	200
Cranberry juice (64 oz. bottle)	3	5	7
Pineapple juice (46 oz. can)	4	6	8
Orange juice (2 qt. carton)	2	4	6
Ginger ale (2 liter bottle)	4	7	9
Almond extract	4 Tbsp.	6 Tbsp.	8 Tbsp.
Oranges, sliced	3	5	7
Bagged ice, (10 lb. bags)	5	7	10
Large ice chest	2	2	3
Clean 5-gallon buckets	2	2	3
Clean 1-gallon buckets	2	2	2
Large spoon (to mix punch)	1	1	1
Matches	1 book	1 book	1 book

Citrus Punch

In the 5-gallon buckets, combine cranberry juice, pineapple juice, orange juice, and almond extract (divided equally among the buckets).

Just before the reception, add ginger ale to the mix.

Because the 5-gallon buckets will be too heavy and cumbersome to lift easily, fill the 1-gallon buckets with punch and pour into the punch fountain. (The fountain will be waiting for you at the reception site.) Use the smaller buckets to refill the fountain during the reception. Store buckets of punch under the table.

Slice oranges ¼" thick and float them on top of the punch.

Always add ice directly to the punch fountain, not to the 1- or 5-gallon buckets. Store ice (in an ice chest) under the table.

Ultimate Reception Room

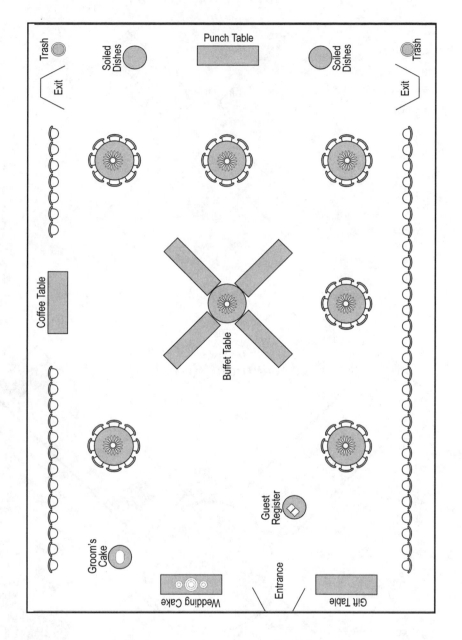

Buffet Table Leather Leaf Placement

Buffet Table for Ultimate Reception

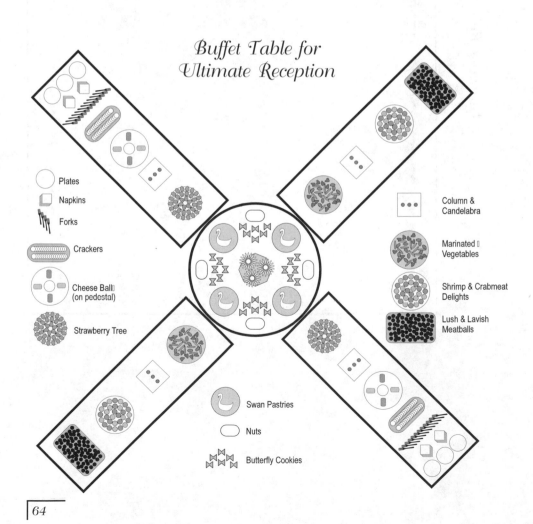

◯ Plates

▢ Napkins

🍴 Forks

Crackers

Cheese Ball (on pedestal)

Strawberry Tree

⬛ Column & Candelabra

Marinated Vegetables

Shrimp & Crabmeat Delights

Lush & Lavish Meatballs

Swan Pastries

◯ Nuts

Butterfly Cookies

Ultimate Wedding Cake Table

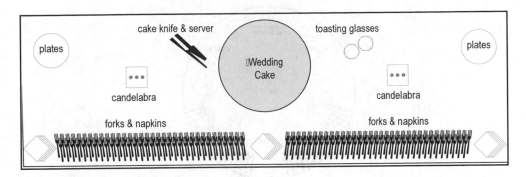

Ultimate Punch Table

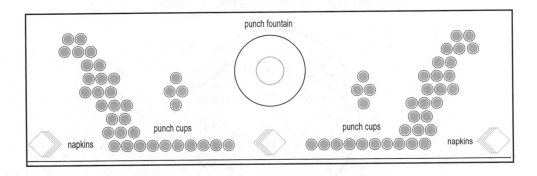

Ultimate Coffee Service Table

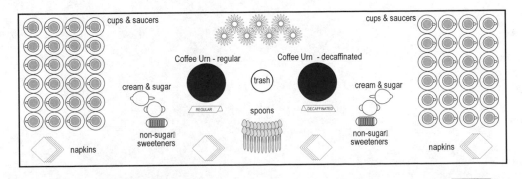

Ultimate Groom's Cake Table

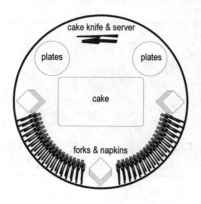

Ultimate Guest Registry Table

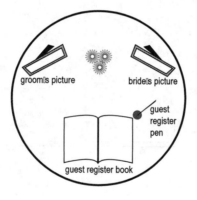

 *Chapter 4*

The Elegant Reception

Are you looking for a reception plan that's jazzier than the Basic but not quite as elaborate as the Ultimate? One that will wow your guests but not overwhelm them by the sheer magnificence of it all? Take a look at this one.

The Elegant Reception features a nice variety of impressive hors d'oeuvres that look terrific and taste even better. Whether your reception will be in the afternoon or right at dinner time, none of your guests will leave the party hungry. And, like a basic black dress, this plan is versatile enough for a black-tie reception or a more casual affair.

Depending on the number of guests you're inviting, you'll need 12 to 17 reliable friends to help you pull the Elegant Reception together. Every menu item in this plan should be made at least a day or two ahead of time (except the punch and coffee, which will be put together at the reception), so none of your helpers will have to worry about being able to make it to the church on time! Only your Setup/Take-Down Team will be busy on the big day—but not so busy that they'll miss the "I do's."

The Menu

Roast Beef Rollups
Salmon-Stuffed Zucchini Boats
Miniature Tropical Fruit Skewers
Heart-Shaped Strawberry Cheese Balls
Raspberry Pastry Puffs
Spiced Nuts
Citrus Fruit Punch
Freshly Brewed Regular and Decaffeinated Coffee

The Helpers

You'll need 10 teams—12 to 17 people—to help with this reception. Detailed job descriptions for each team are provided later in this chapter, but here's a quick summary of the type of help you're looking for.

Setup/Take-Down Team: Do you have two or three non-cook friends who want to help with your reception? Give them this job! They need to be able to lift—or at least drag—tables and chairs and dress your hall up with linens and whatever decorations you provide.

Roast Beef Rollups Team: There is no cooking involved in this job; the only culinary skills this team of one or two needs is cutting, rolling, and poking. You might want to look for a married couple or two roommates for this job; they live in the same household and share a kitchen so they won't have to transport cooking utensils and supplies.

Salmon-Stuffed Zucchini Boats Team: This is another job that requires little in the way of cooking ability. You might want to recruit two people from different households; they're going to need a lot of refrigerator space. (If your guest list isn't too large, you'll only need one helper for this job.)

Miniature Tropical Fruit Skewers Team: One or two people can easily handle this job that requires only the ability to grip a knife. Look for helpers who have plenty of refrigerator space available.

Heart-Shaped Strawberry Cheeseball Team: Simple, simple, simple! Only one helper—and very little refrigerator space—needed for this job. This person also has the honor of cutting and serving the wedding cake.

Raspberry Pastry Puffs Team: If you only have a couple of friends who know how to cook, give them this job. The recipe's not difficult, but it's more involved than any of the others in this plan. Look for people from two different households so they'll have enough refrigerator space between them.

Spiced Nuts Team: This is another easy job for one person, no matter how many guests you have. These trays can be made up to six weeks in advance and don't require much freezer space for storage. This person also has the honor of cutting and serving the groom's cake.

Citrus Punch Team: Make sure the one or two people you get for this job can lift buckets of punch and bags of ice without straining something. The punch recipe is easy to follow and hard to mess up, even for the most novice of novices.

Coffee Team: Don't worry about finding a culinary genius for this job—it's coffee, for Pete's sake! One or two people can handle this one.

The Hardware

In addition to recruiting the people who will help you with your reception, you'll need to rent or purchase the following items. Before whipping out your credit card, however, ask your reception site representative if he or she can provide any of the items free of charge or at a discount. You may also be able to borrow many of the items from friends and family members and save yourself some serious money. See Chapter 9 for complete information on renting or otherwise acquiring these supplies.

Included in this list are white table linens, centerpieces, floral arrangements, and candelabras. These are staples at traditional wedding receptions, but you may want to use some other type of decorations. Chapter 8 is packed with decorating ideas you may want to consider.

Number of guests:	100	150	200
60" round tables	7	7	7
8' x 30" banquet tables	8	8	8
36" round tables	4	4	4
Folding chairs	100	150	200
120" round white tablecloths	7	7	7
90" round white tablecloths	4	4	4
54" x 120" white tablecloths	8	8	8
21' white skirting segments	8	8	8
5-gallon punch fountain	1	1	1
5-oz. glass punch cups	125	175	225
90-cup stainless steel coffee urns	2	2	2
Coffee cups	75	100	125
Coffee saucers	75	100	125
Sugar bowls	4	4	4
Creamers	2	2	2
Spoons	75	100	100
Forks	275	400	550
8" glass plates	275	400	550
5-branch candelabras	6	6	6
16" white tapered candles	30	30	30

Number of guests:	100	150	200
Floral centerpiece for buffet	1	1	1
Floral centerpieces for guest tables	7	7	7
Floral centerpiece for coffee table	1	1	1
Floral centerpiece for guest registry table	1	1	1
18"h x 11"w white columns (from a craft store or garden center)	5	5	5
Wedding cake	1	1	1
Groom's cake	1	1	1
Cake knife and server	2 sets	2 sets	2 sets
Engraved napkins	425	625	725
Guest book and pen	1 set	1 set	1 set
Toasting glasses	1 set	1 set	1 set

*Note: Have your rentals delivered the day **before** the reception. You don't want your setup team waiting around for a delivery. All items should be there when the team arrives so that they can immediately start setting up.*

Reception Team Job Descriptions

Team 1: Setup/Take-Down Team

Helper #1 _____

Helper #2 _____

Helper #3 _____

Reception Coordinator _____

Reception Location _____

Time of Ceremony _____

Number of Guests _____

Responsibilities

❧ Clean out two large plastic trash cans for use at the reception. Because these will be seen by guests, try to find cans that are presentable. Be sure to bring about a half dozen trash can liners.

❧ Arrive at the reception site about four hours before the ceremony to arrange tables and chairs in their designated locations (see the Elegant Reception Room diagram on page 86).

❧ Place tablecloths and skirting on tables as follows:
- Eight 8' x 30" tables (wedding cake, gift, punch, and four buffet tables) and 54" x 120" tablecloths. Clip skirting on *before* laying the tablecloth on the table.
- Seven 60" round tables (center buffet and six guest tables) and 120" round tablecloths. No skirting required.
- Four 36" round tables (guest registry, groom's cake, and two soiled dish tables) and 90" round tablecloths. No skirting required.

❧ If more than one color will be used on the tables, the bride will let you know how the linens should be arranged.

❧ The bride will provide items such as dishes, silverware, punch fountain, and centerpieces and have them delivered to the site. Using the diagrams for the Buffet Table, Wedding Cake Table, Punch Table, Coffee Table, Groom's Cake Table, and Guest Registry Table (see pages 87 to 89), arrange the items on the tables.

❧ During the reception, help keep the area neat and clean. Keep an eye on the trash cans and replace full liners when needed.

❧ At the end of the reception, help with clean up and return rented items to the location of the room where they were delivered.

Team 2: Roast Beef Rollups Team

Helper #1: _____

Helper #2: _____

Reception Coordinator _____

Reception Location _____

Time of Ceremony _____

Number of Guests _____

Responsibilities

 ▬ The day before the reception, make the Roast Beef Rollups and Sour Cream and Horseradish Sauce according to the recipes on page 73. Because these need to be refrigerated, you might want to clean out your fridge ahead of time so you'll have plenty of room to store them.

 ▬ Arrive at the reception site no more than an hour before the ceremony and place the trays of Roast Beef Rollups and tongs on the buffet tables as shown on the Buffet Table diagram on page 87. Place the bowls of Sour Cream and Horseradish Sauce in the center of each tray and put two spoons in each bowl. Your extra Rollups should be refrigerated at the reception site. If no refrigerator is available, store them in a shady, cool spot out of direct sunlight.

 ▬ Keep an eye on your trays during the reception and replenish them when necessary.

 ▬ At the end of the reception, help with clean up.

Shopping List

Number of guests	100	150	200
For Roast Beef Rollups			
Roast beef (2 oz. slices)	18 lbs.	27 lbs.	36 lbs.
Kosher pickle spears	144	216	288
Sliced pimentos (7 oz jar)	1	2	2
Whole stuffed green olives	144	216	288
Frilly toothpicks	144	216	288
20" trays (glass or silver)	2	2	2
Tongs	4	4	4

Number of guests	100	150	200
For Sour Cream and Horseradish Sauce			
Sour cream	2 cups	3 cups	4 cups
Prepared horseradish	½ cup	¾ cup	1 cup
Dijon mustard	½ cup	¾ cup	1 cup
Chopped chives	sprinkle	sprinkle	sprinkle
Spoons	4	4	4

Roast Beef Rollups

Visit your grocery store's deli department and ask for the required number of 2 oz. slices of roast beef. Be sure to ask them to cut the slices all the same size.

Lay each roast beef slice flat and place a pickle spear on top. Roll the beef slice around the pickle so that you end up with a long, skinny roll.

With a toothpick in hand, stab through an olive then a pimento strip. Stick the garnished toothpick into the rollup.

Arrange rollups on the trays, leaving an open space in the middle for the bowl of Sour Cream and Horseradish Sauce. Cover tightly with plastic wrap, and refrigerate.

Sour Cream and Horseradish Sauce

Whip sour cream, horseradish sauce, and Dijon mustard together. Cover and refrigerate.

Sprinkle chopped chives on top of sauce before serving.

Team 3: Salmon-Stuffed Zucchini Boats

Helper #1 _____

Helper #2 _____

Reception Coordinator _____

Reception Location _____

Time of Ceremony _____

Number of Guests _____

Responsibilities

- The day before the reception, make the Zucchini Boats according to the recipe on page 75. Because these need to be refrigerated, you might want to clean out your fridge ahead of time so you'll have plenty of room to store them.

- Arrive at the reception site no more than an hour before the ceremony and place the trays of Zucchini Boats and tongs on the buffet tables as shown on the Buffet Table diagram on page 87. Extra Boats should be refrigerated, but if no refrigerator is available, store them in a shady, cool spot out of direct sunlight.

- Keep an eye on your trays during the reception and replenish them when necessary.

- At the end of the reception, help with clean up.

Shopping List

Number of guests	100	150	200
Salmon, cooked and flaked	8 lbs.	12 lbs.	16 lbs.
Mayonnaise	2 cups	3 cups	4 cups
Lime juice	½ cup	¾ cup	1 cup
Dill, finely diced	1 cup	1½ cups	2 cups
White pepper	2 tsp.	3 tsp.	4 tsp.
Salt	2 tsp.	3 tsp.	4 tsp.
Cayenne pepper	1 tsp.	1½ tsp.	2 tsp.
Celery, finely diced	5 cups	7½ cups	10 cups
Red pepper, finely diced	1 cup	1½ cups	2 cups
Fresh zucchini	17	26	34
Poppy seed	1 jar	1 jar	1 jar
Fresh parsley, bunches	2	3	4
20" trays (glass or silver)	2	2	2
Tongs	4	4	4

Salmon-Stuffed Zucchini Boats

Whip the mayonnaise, lime juice, dill, pepper, salt, and cayenne pepper in a large bowl. Add the salmon and mix well. With a rubber spatula, fold in the celery and diced red pepper.

Cover with plastic wrap and refrigerate.

Cut the ends off of the zucchini (approximately ½"). Cut each zucchini into three equal parts so you have three round cylinders. Split the three cylinders in half lengthwise to create six zucchini boats.

Scoop out the seeds in the middle of the boats, leaving about ¼" on each side intact. Sprinkle the boats with salt, turn them upside down on paper towels, and allow to drain for 20 minutes. Turn the boats right side up and stuff with the salmon mixture. Garnish with a sprinkle of poppy seed and a sprig of parsley.

Arrange the garnished Zucchini Boats on your trays, cover with plastic wrap, and refrigerate.

Put any extras on cookie sheets and cover with plastic wrap (use these to replenish the trays during the reception).

Team 5: Miniature Tropical Fruit Skewers Team

Helper #1 _____

Helper #2 _____

Reception Coordinator _____

Reception Location _____

Time of Ceremony _____

Number of Guests _____

Responsibilities

❧ The day before the reception, make the Fruit Skewers and Dipping Sauce according to the recipes on pages 77. Because these need to be refrigerated, you might want to clean out your fridge ahead of time so you'll have plenty of room to store them.

❧ Arrive at the reception site no more than an hour before the ceremony and place the trays of Fruit Skewers and tongs on the buffet tables as shown on the Buffet Table diagram on page 87. Place two spoons in each sauce bowl. Your extra Skewers should be refrigerated at the reception site. If no refrigerator is available, store them in a shady, cool spot out of direct sunlight.

❧ Keep an eye on your trays during the reception and replenish them when necessary.

❧ At the end of the reception, help with clean up.

Shopping List

Number of guests	100	150	200
For Tropical Fruit Skewers			
Cantaloupe	4	6	8
Honeydew	3	5	7
Pineapple	8	12	16
Strawberries	200 (18 pts.)	300 (24 pts.)	400 (36 pts.)
6" Wooden Skewers	100	150	200
20" trays (glass or silver)	2	2	2
Tongs	4	4	4

Number of guests	100	150	200
For Dipping Sauce			
Sour cream	4 cups	6 cups	8 cups
Light brown sugar	1 lb.	1½ lb.	2 lbs.
Cinnamon	4 Tbsp.	6 Tbsp.	8 Tbsp.
Kahlua	1 oz.	1½ oz.	2 oz.
Bowls	2	2	2
Spoons	4	4	4

Dipping Sauce

Whip the sour cream, brown sugar, cinnamon, and kahlua together in a small mixing bowl. Separate the sauce into two small glass bowls. These bowls will be placed in the center of the trays and should be just large enough to hold the entire amount of sauce.

Miniature Tropical Fruit Skewers

Peel away the rinds from the cantaloupe and honeydew melons. Split melons in half and remove the seeds. Cut each melon into ½" cubes.

Cut off the tops of all the strawberries.

Cut the tops and bottoms off the pineapples and peel away the rinds. Split each pineapple in half lengthwise. Slicing at a V-shape angle, cut out the core. Cut pineapple into ½" cubes.

Slide two pieces of each fruit onto each skewer.

Place the sauce bowls in the middle of the trays and arrange the fruit around them until the trays are full. You may have to stack the skewers on top of each other to fit them all on the trays. If you have extras, place them on a cookie sheet and use them to replenish the trays during the reception.

Cover trays tightly with plastic wrap and refrigerate.

Team 5: Heart-Shaped Strawberry Cheeseballs Team

Helper #1 _____

Reception Coordinator _____

Reception Location _____

Time of Ceremony _____

Number of Guests _____

Responsibilities

- The day before or early on the day of the reception, make the cheeseballs according to the recipe that follows.

- Arrive at the reception no more than an hour before the ceremony and place the cheeseballs on the buffet tables as shown on the Buffet Table diagram on page 87. Place two knives on each tray.

- Keep an eye on your trays during the reception and replenish the crackers when they begin to run low.

- Help cut and serve the wedding cake.

- At the end of the reception, help with clean up.

Shopping List

Number of guests	100	150	200
Cream cheese	4 lbs.	6 lbs.	8 lbs.
Pecans, chopped	3 lbs.	4½ lbs.	6 lbs.
Strawberry preserves	16 oz.	24 oz.	32 oz.
Wheat Thin crackers	4 boxes	6 boxes	8 boxes
Knives	4	4	4
20" trays (glass or silver)	2	2	2

Heart-Shaped Strawberry Cheeseballs

Mix the pecans and cream cheese together well. If your mixer can't handle the entire amount, combine half of the cream cheese with half of the pecans. In another bowl, combine the remaining cream cheese and pecans.

Form two balls and place one in the center of each tray. With your hands, shape each ball into a flat heart about ½" inch thick. Wrap the trays with plastic wrap and refrigerate.

At the reception site, spread the preserves over the top and sides of the hearts. Arrange crackers around the hearts.

Team 6: Raspberry Pastry Puffs Team

Helper #1 _____

Helper #2 _____

Reception Coordinator _____

Reception Location _____

Time of Ceremony _____

Number of Guests _____

Responsibilities

- The day before the reception, make the Raspberry Pastry Puffs according to the recipes on page 80. Because these need to be refrigerated, you might want to clean out your fridge ahead of time so you'll have plenty of room to store them.

- Arrive at the reception site no more than an hour before the ceremony and place the trays of Puffs and tongs on the buffet tables as shown on the Buffet Table diagram on page 87. Extra Puffs should be refrigerated at the reception site. If no refrigerator is available, store them in a shady, cool spot out of direct sunlight.

- Keep an eye on your trays during the reception and replenish them when necessary.

- At the end of the reception, help with clean up.

Shopping List

Number of guests	100	150	200
For Pastry Puffs			
Water	8 cups	12 cups	16 cups
Margarine	4 cups	6 cups	8 cups
All-purpose flour	8 cups	12 cups	16 cups
Salt	1½ tsp.	2¼ tsp.	3 tsp.
Fresh large eggs	3 dozen	4½ dozen	6 dozen
Pastry bag	1	1	1
Raspberry Pastry Filling			
Whipping cream	9 cups	14 cups	18 cups
Powdered sugar (sifted)	3½ cups	5¼ cups	7 cups
Fresh raspberries	18 pints	27 pints	36 pints
Fresh mint leaves, bunches	3	4	5
20" trays (glass or silver)	4	4	4
Tongs	8	8	8

Pastry Puffs

Bring water and margarine to a rolling boil. If you don't have large enough pots to handle this task, divide the recipe into equal parts and use two or more pots.

Add flour and salt and stir vigorously over medium heat until the mixture separates from the sides of the pot and a smooth ball forms (about one minute).

Remove from heat and allow to cool for 20 minutes.

Slowly add eggs one at a time while beating vigorously with an electric mixer or a wooden spoon.

Without a tip inserted, load your pastry bag with the dough and pipe out golf ball-sized pastry balls 2½" apart on an ungreased cookie sheet. If you are not familiar with using a pastry bag, use a large spoon and dip out golf ball-sized pastry balls to place on the cookie sheet.

Bake at 400 degrees for 30-35 minutes or until golden brown.

Remove from oven and allow 25 minutes to cool down.

Raspberry Filling

Beat the whipping cream until it's slightly stiff. Slowly add powdered sugar while whipping until soft peaks are formed.

Using a rubber spatula, fold in about three-quarters of the raspberries.

Cut off the tops of the baked pastries and fill with the raspberry cream. Sprinkle a few of the remaining raspberries on top and replace the cap.

Arrange the pastries on the trays, cover with plastic wrap, and refrigerate. If you have extras, place them on a cookie sheet, cover with plastic wrap, and refrigerate. You'll use these to replenish the trays during the reception.

Sprinkle mint leaves on puffs after placing the trays on the buffet table at the reception.

Team 7: Spiced Nuts Team

Helper #1 _____

Reception Coordinator _____

Reception Location _____

Time of Ceremony _____

Number of Guests _____

Responsibilities

❧ Make Spiced Nuts according to the recipe that follows several days before the reception.

❧ Arrive 15 to 30 minutes before the ceremony and place nuts in their designated places on the buffet table (see Buffet Table diagram on page 87).

❧ Help cut and serve the groom's cake.

❧ At the end of the reception, help with clean up.

Shopping List

Number of guests	100	150	200
Walnuts	1 lb.	1½ lbs.	2 lbs.
Pecans	1 lb.	1½ lbs.	2 lbs.
Margarine	1 cup	1½ cups	2 cups
Powdered sugar	3 cups	4½ cups	6 cups
Cinnamon	2 Tbsp.	3 Tbsp.	4 Tbsp.
Ground cloves	4 Tbsp.	6 Tbsp.	8 Tbsp.
Ground nutmeg	4 Tbsp.	6 Tbsp.	8 Tbsp.

Spiced Nuts

Spiced Nuts can be made up to six weeks in advance and kept in your freezer until ready for use.

Place the margarine and nuts in a large pot on top of the stove. Cook over low to medium heat for 15 to 20 minutes, stirring constantly. Nuts should be cooked until lightly browned. Be careful not to burn them.

Pour browned nuts onto a paper towel-lined cookie sheet and drain well. In a separate bowl, mix together the spices. Pour nuts into the bowl of spices and toss until they're well coated. Pour the coated nuts into a mesh strainer and shake off excess spices. Place coated nuts into baggies and freeze.

Team 8: Citrus Punch Team

Helper #1 _____

Helper #2 _____

Reception Coordinator _____

Reception Location _____

Time of Ceremony _____

Number of Guests _____

Responsibilities

- Gather all ingredients for the punch and arrive at the reception site one hour before the wedding. Decide ahead of time where you're going to get the ice and pick it up on your way to the reception site. Make the punch at the reception site according to the recipe on page 83.

- Fill the punch fountain with ice and punch and keep it replenished during the reception. The fountain will be waiting for you at the hall, but you'll need to bring an extension cord (see Shopping List) in case the fountain's cord won't easily reach an outlet.

- Light all candles on the buffet table right before the reception begins.

- At the end of the reception, help with clean up.

Shopping List

Number of guests	100	150	200
Cranberry juice (64 oz. bottle)	3	5	7
Pineapple juice (46 oz. can)	4	6	8
Orange juice (2 qt. carton)	2	4	6
Ginger ale (2 liter bottle)	4	7	9
Almond extract	4 Tbsp.	6 Tbsp.	8 Tbsp.
Orange slices	3 oranges	5 oranges	7 oranges
Bagged ice (10 lb. bags)	5	7	10
Large ice chest	2	2	3
Clean 5-gallon buckets	2	2	3
Clean 1-gallon buckets	2	2	2
Large spoon (to mix punch)	1	1	1
Matches	1 book	1 book	1 book

Citrus Punch

In the 5-gallon buckets, combine cranberry juice, pineapple juice, orange juice, and almond extract (divided equally among the buckets).

Just before the reception, add ginger ale to the mix.

Because the 5-gallon buckets will be too heavy and cumbersome to lift easily, fill the 1-gallon buckets with punch and pour into the punch fountain. (The fountain will be waiting for you at the reception site.) Use the smaller buckets to refill the fountain during the reception. Store buckets of punch under the table.

Slice oranges ¼" thick and float them on top of the punch.

Always add ice directly to the punch fountain, not to the 1- or 5-gallon buckets. Store ice (in an ice chest) under the table.

Team 9: Coffee Team

Helper #1 _____

Helper #2 _____

Reception Coordinator _____

Reception Location _____

Time of Ceremony _____

Number of Guests _____

Responsibilities

❧ Make small placards or signs for regular and decaffeinated coffee. You may want to make these on your computer or write them in calligraphy.

❧ The coffee will take 30 minutes to an hour to brew. Arrive at the reception site in plenty of time for the coffee to be ready by the beginning of the reception. The coffee urns will be waiting for you at the reception site.

❧ Using the Coffee Table diagram on page 88, place the small bowls and creamers in their assigned spots. Fill half the bowls with sugar and the other half with sweetener packets. Fill the creamers with half-and-half. Place the coffee signs/placards in front of the appropriate coffee urn. Place back-up supplies under the table.

❧ During the reception, keep an eye on the coffee table and replenish sugar, cream, and so forth as necessary.

❧ At the end of the reception, help with clean up.

Shopping List

Number of guests	100	150	200
Regular coffee	10 oz.	15 oz.	20 oz.
Decaffeinated coffee	10 oz.	15 oz.	20 oz.
Water per urn	50 cups	75 cups	90 cups
Sugar	1 lb.	1½ lbs.	2 lbs.
Sweet & Low (Packets)	50	75	100
Equal (Packets)	25	35	50
Cream (half-and-half)	2 qts.	3 qts.	4 qts.
Glass bowls (softball size)	6	6	6
Regular and Decaffeinated signs	1ea.	1ea.	1ea.
12' three-pronged extension cords	2	2	2

Coffee

At the reception site, make sure that the coffee table is located near electrical outlets. You may have to move the table closer to an outlet if you don't have easy access. Use your extension cords if necessary.

Remove the lids, filters, and stems from the coffee pots. Fill the pots to the correct water line (look for lines inside the pots). Reinsert the stems and filters. Fill the filters with the desired amount of coffee (read the labels on the coffee can to find out how much coffee to measure into the filters). Secure the lids and turn the coffee urns on. The coffee will take from 30 minutes to an hour to brew.

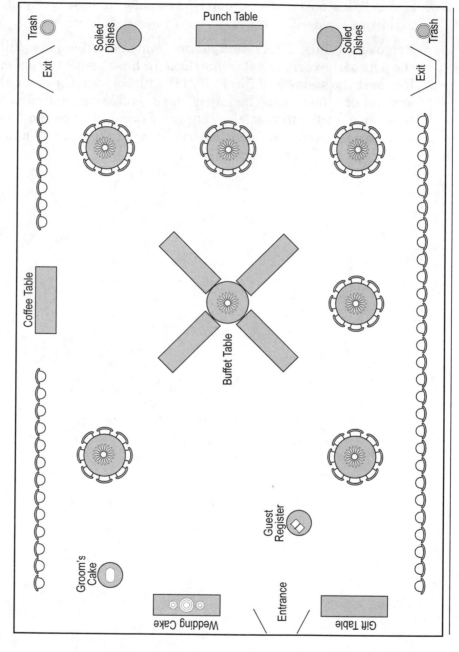

Elegant Reception Room

Buffet Table for Elegant Reception

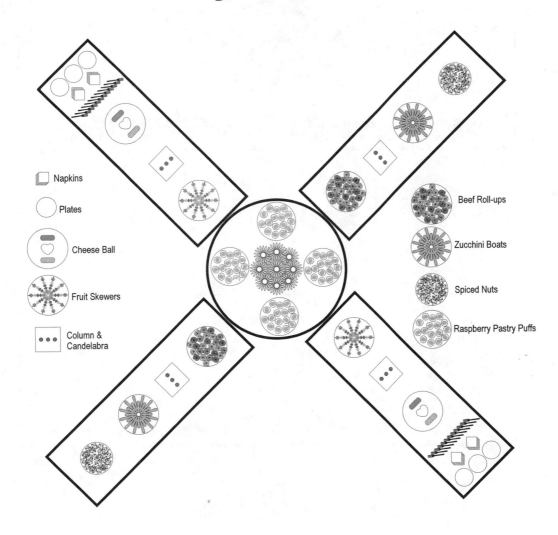

Napkins

Plates

Cheese Ball

Fruit Skewers

Column & Candelabra

Beef Roll-ups

Zucchini Boats

Spiced Nuts

Raspberry Pastry Puffs

Elegant Wedding Cake Table

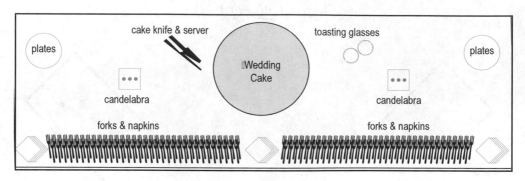

Elegant Punch Table

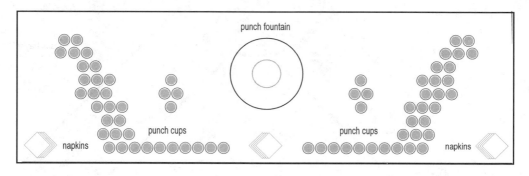

Elegant Coffee Service Table

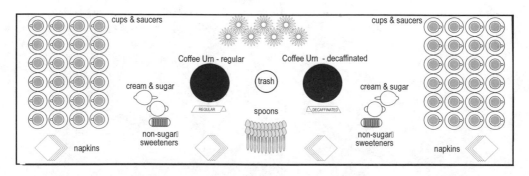

Elegant Groom's Cake Table

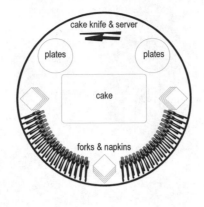

Elegant Guest Registry Table

 *Chapter 5*

The Backyard Barbecue Reception

What's the most fun you can have on a wedding night if you're not the bride and groom? A backyard barbecue reception! This reception plan is perfect if you want to throw an informal celebration with lots of fun and loads of good food.

Depending on the number of guests you're inviting, you'll need 13 to 21 reliable friends to help you with the Backyard Barbecue Reception. Be sure to discuss logistics with your Barbecued Chicken team members early on—decide together if they'll grill the chicken ahead of time or at the reception. If they want to cook at the reception, you'll have to provide several grills.

As for the rest of the teams, it's a piece of cake! No members of your teams will be too tired from making their menu items that they won't be able join in on a Cotton-Eye Joe or a wild game of volleyball. If you want a maximum of fun with a minimum of work, this is the reception plan for you.

The Menu

Barbecued Chicken
World's Best Deviled Eggs
Flame-Roasted Corn on the Cob
Oughta-Be-Illegal Green Beans
Southern-Style Pork and Beans
Mother Frye's Potato Salad
Carolina Coleslaw
Bread and Butter Pickles
Yeast Rolls and Butter
Homemade Vanilla Ice Cream
Iced Tea and Coffee

The Helpers

You'll need 12 teams to help with this reception. Detailed job descriptions for each team are provided later in this chapter, but here's a quick summary of the type of help you're looking for.

Setup/Take-Down Team: You'll need two or three people to set up the tables and chairs before the reception and then take everything down when it's over. Recruit your brawniest friends for this one—some heavy lifting is required. This team will also put out any tablecloths, centerpieces, and equipment (such as a coffee urn) you provide.

Barbecue Chicken Team: Everyone has a couple of buddies who love to grill—these are the folks you want on this team. Be sure to plan whether they'll cook the chicken beforehand or at the reception so you can provide the grills if needed.

Deviled Eggs Team: Do you have a friend or two whose only culinary ability is boiling water? This is the job for them! If they can boil water and wield a spoon, they're qualified.

Corn on the Cob Team: Here's another one for the cooking-impaired. The most difficult part of this job is pulling the husks and silk off the corn. This team of one or two gets the honor of helping to cut the wedding cake.

Green Beans Team: The hardest job for this team is opening six to 18 cans of green beans! This team (one or two people) also gets the honor of cutting and serving the groom's cake if one is provided.

Pork and Beans Team: There's nothing complicated about this job either. One or two people can easily handle this job, regardless of the number of guests you invite to the reception.

Potato Salad Team: This is another job for one or two people who can boil water, but it also requires a bit of chopping and whipping abilitly.

Coleslaw Team: Look for a friend or two with food processors—this job requires a good bit of chopping and dicing, but the recipe's a snap.

Yeast Rolls and Pickles Team: Absolutely no cooking skill or experience whatsoever is required for this person. The only criteria he or she needs to meet is an ability to turn on an oven and set a timer.

Homemade Ice Cream Team: This is the only team (one to two people) who will need special equipment—he or she should have (or know where to borrow) an ice cream maker. If they already own one, they're probably well versed on its use so their job will be easy.

If they've never used one before, it's not exactly rocket science, so they shouldn't have any trouble with it either. This team dips the ice cream as the cake is being served.

Iced Tea and Coffee Team: It doesn't come much easier than this—unless you count the Deviled Egg Team's job! One person can handle beverage duty alone, but may need help lifting the full coffee urns during setup.

The Hardware

In addition to recruiting the people who will help you with your reception, you'll need to rent or purchase the items that follow. Before whipping out your credit card, however, ask your reception site representative if he or she can provide any of the items free of charge or at a discount. You may also be able to borrow many of the items from friends and family members and save yourself some serious money. See Chapter 9 for complete information on renting or otherwise acquiring these supplies.

Think of this plan as an organized potluck supper. Because informality is the name of the game, you can forget about things like table skirts and elaborate floral centerpieces if you want—checkered tablecloths and canning jars filled with wildflowers will be perfect. (For other unique decorating ideas, see Chapter 8.) Paper plates and plastic flatware and glasses make clean up a breeze. And don't worry about rounding up matching serving dishes and utensils. Just ask your reception team to serve their menu items in the bowls, platters, baskets, and trays they already have. (In case you'd rather rent dishes and linens and dress things up, quantities are included in the list below.)

Number of guests	25	50	75
8' x 30" banquet tables	8	10	16
54" x 120" white tablecloths	8	10	16
21' white skirting segments	5	5	6
White Samsonite chairs	25	50	75
12" white china dinner plates	25	50	75
5-oz. white china fruit bowls	25	50	75
Dinner forks	25	50	75
Dinner knives	25	50	75
Dinner spoons	25	50	75
12-oz. water goblets	25	50	75
20" x 20" white linen napkins	25	50	75
White coffee cups	25	50	75

Number of guests	25	50	75
White coffee saucers	25	50	75
Salt and pepper shakers	4 sets	6 sets	10 sets
Glass sugar bowls	4	6	10
Glass creamers	4	6	10
3-gallon tea dispenser	1	1	1
25-cup coffee urns	2	0	0
50-cup coffee urns	0	2	0
90-cup coffee urns	0	0	2
Floral centerpiece for buffet	1	1	1
Floral centerpieces for guest tables	3	5	9
8" glass plates	25	50	75
Cake knife and server	1 set	1 set	1 set
Wedding cake	1	1	1
Engraved cocktail napkins	65	125	200
Toasting glasses	1 set	1 set	1 set

*Note: Have your rentals delivered the day **before** the reception. You don't want your setup team waiting around for a delivery. All items should be there when the team arrives so that they can immediately start setting up.*

Reception Team Job Descriptions

Team 1: Setup/Take-Down Team

Helper #1 _____

Helper #2 _____

Helper #3 _____

Reception Coordinator _____

Reception Location _____

Time of Ceremony _____

Number of Guests _____

Responsibilities

- Clean out two large plastic trash cans for use at the reception. Because these will be seen by guests, try to find cans that are presentable. Be sure to bring about a half dozen trash can liners.

- Arrive at the reception site about three hours before the ceremony to arrange the tables and chairs in their designated locations (see the Backyard Barbecue Reception diagrams on pages 113 to 115).

- The bride will let you know whether she's planning to use tablecloths; if it's an outdoor reception with picnic benches, she might skip them or she may decide to use tablecloths only on the serving and other utility tables. Regardless of what she decides, she'll let you know and provide any linens you'll need.

- If the bride decides to use table linens as outlined in this chapter, place them on the tables as follows:
  - **For 25 guests:** Four 8' x 30" tables (wedding cake, drink station, and buffet tables) and 54" x 120" tablecloths. Clip skirting on *before* laying the tablecloth on the table. Four 8' x 30" tables (guest tables) and 54" x 120" tablecloths—no skirting required.
  - **For 50 guests:** Four 8' x 30" tables (wedding cake, drink station, and buffet tables) and 54" x 120" tablecloths. Clip skirting on *before* laying the tablecloth on the table. Six 8' x 30" tables (54" x 120" tablecloths) for guests—no skirting required.
  - **For 75 guests:** Six 8' x 30" tables (wedding cake, drink station, and buffet tables) and 54" x 120" tablecloths. Clip skirting on *before* laying the tablecloth on the table. Ten 8' x 30" tables (54" x 120" tablecloths) for guests—no skirting required.

❧ The bride will provide items such as dishes (paper, plastic, or china), utensils, and centerpieces and have them delivered to the reception site. Using the diagrams for the Buffet Table, Place Setting, Wedding Cake Table, and Drink Station (see pages 116 and 117), arrange the items on the appropriate tables.

❧ During the reception, help keep the area neat and clean. Keep an eye on the trash cans and replace the liners when they get full.

❧ At the end of the reception, help with clean up and arrange rented items for easy pick up.

Team 2: Barbecued Chicken Team

Helper #1 _____

Helper #2 _____

Helper #3 _____

Reception Coordinator _____

Reception Location _____

Time of Ceremony _____

Number of Guests _____

Responsibilities

  ❧ Decide when and where you want to grill the chicken. You have three options.

- Plan A: Grill the chicken the day before the reception, cover with tin foil, and refrigerate overnight. On the day of the reception, reheat them in your oven just prior to the reception.
- Plan B: Cook the chicken at the reception site and serve them hot off the grill. If you go with Plan B, you will need to supply your own grill(s) or make arrangements with the bride to have them available at the reception site.
- Plan C: Cook the chicken in the oven the day before, then reheat them right before the reception.

  ❧ Before the wedding begins, take the chicken to the reception site. If you've precooked it, place the chicken (covered with tin foil) in a warm oven. Set the chicken in the designated spot on the buffet table right before the reception begins. If you've decided to grill the chicken at the reception, refrigerate the uncooked chicken. As soon as the wedding ceremony is over, high tail it to the reception site and fire up the grill(s). The chicken will take about 1½ hours to cook—roughly the amount of time most photographers detain the wedding party after the ceremony to take pictures.

  ❧ At the end of the reception, help with clean up.

Shopping List

Number of guests	25	50	75
Ketchup	3 cups	4½ cups	6 cups
Orange juice	3 cups	4½ cups	6 cups
Honey	1 cup	1½ cups	2 cups
Soy sauce	½ cup	¾ cup	1 cup
Garlic cloves (chopped fine)	6	9	12
Salt	1 Tbsp.	1½ Tbsp.	2 Tbsp.
Pepper	2 tsp.	3 tsp.	4 tsp.
Chicken breast halves	25	50	75
Serving trays	2	4	6
Tongs	4	8	12

Barbecue Chicken

In a large bowl, combine all ingredients except the chicken. Mix well.

Place the chicken breasts (skin side up) in large, shallow pans and pour the barbecue marinade over them. Cover the pans with foil and marinate overnight in the refrigerator.

Preheat grills to 300 degrees. Place the chicken breasts on the grill (skin side down). Cook slowly for 45 minutes (turning occasionally and basting with remaining marinade) or until done.

If grills are not available, you can bake the chicken in the oven (covered) at 300 degrees for 1½ hours or until done.

Team 3: Deviled Eggs Team

Helper #1 _____

Helper #2 _____

Reception Coordinator _____

Reception Location _____

Time of Ceremony _____

Number of Guests _____

Responsibilities

❧ Make the eggs the day before the reception, but don't garnish with the paprika and parsley until right before you leave for the reception. Because the eggs need to be refrigerated, clean out your fridge ahead of time so you'll have room to store them.

❧ Arrive at the reception site no more than 30 minutes before the wedding and place the trays of eggs on the buffet tables as shown on the Buffet Table diagram on page 116. Your extra eggs should be refrigerated at the reception site. If no refrigerator is available, store them in a shady, cool spot out of direct sunlight.

❧ Replenish the trays when necessary during the reception.

❧ At the end of the reception, help with clean up.

Shopping List

Number of guests	25	50	75
Large fresh eggs	2 dozen	3 dozen	4 dozen
Marzetti (or other) Coleslaw Dressing	1 cup	1½ cups	2 cups
Paprika	sprinkle	sprinkle	sprinkle
20" round trays	1	2	3
Serving spoons	2	4	6

World's Best Deviled Eggs

Boil eggs in water and a splash of white vinegar for 22 minutes. (Vinegar makes eggs easier to peel.) Immediately place the cooked eggs into ice water. When eggs are cool enough to handle, remove the shells and slice in half lengthwise.

Scoop out yolks and place in a large mixing bowl. Add coleslaw dressing and whip until smooth. With a spoon, replace yolk mixture into each egg. Garnish with paprika and/or parsley flakes. Cover loosely with plastic wrap and refrigerate.

Team 4: Corn on the Cob Team

Helper #1 _____

Helper #2 _____

Reception Coordinator _____

Reception Location _____

Time of Ceremony _____

Number of Guests _____

Responsibilities

❧ For the freshest taste possible, cook the corn so that it's ready right before it's time to leave for the ceremony. Cover with foil to keep warm.

❧ Arrive at the reception site no more than 30 minutes before the ceremony and place the corn in the oven to keep warm. If no oven space is available, keep the foil-wrapped corn in a cooler that has no ice in it—this will help it stay warm. Before the reception begins, place your trays of corn in their designated spots on the buffet table (see the Buffet Table diagram on page 116).

❧ Keep your back-up corn in an oven on low heat or in an ice-free cooler. During the reception, keep an eye on your trays and replenish them when necessary.

❧ Help cut and serve the wedding cake.

❧ At the end of the reception, help with clean up.

Shopping List

Number of guests	25	50	75
Medium-sized fresh yellow corn	25	50	75
Salt and pepper	to taste	to taste	to taste
Butter	1½ lbs.	2¼ lbs.	3 lbs.
Large bowls	1	2	3
Tongs	2	4	6

Flame-Roasted Corn on the Cob

Remove the husks and corn silk.

Boil the corn in unsalted water for approximately 30 minutes or until tender. Remove from water and place the corn directly onto a hot grill. Roll the corn around on the grill until grill marks appear. Remove from grill and season with salt, pepper, and butter.

Place on a serving tray or platter and cover with foil until time to serve.

Team 5: Oughta-Be-Illegal Green Beans Team

Helper #1 _____

Helper #2 _____

Reception Coordinator _____

Reception Location _____

Time of Ceremony _____

Number of Guests _____

Responsibilities

- Make the beans early on the day of the wedding. (Or you can make them the day before the wedding and refrigerate overnight. Reheat them right before leaving for the wedding and cover the bowl with foil.)

- Arrive at the reception site no more than 30 minutes before the ceremony begins. Place the beans in the oven to keep warm. If no oven space is available, keep the foil-wrapped bowl in a cooler that has no ice in it—this will help them stay warm. Before the reception begins, place your bowl(s) of beans in their designated spots on the buffet table (see the Buffet Table diagram on page 116 for placement).

- Keep your back-up beans in an oven on low heat or in an ice-free cooler. During the reception, keep an eye on your beans and replenish them, if necessary.

- Help cut and serve the groom's cake if one is provided.

- At the end of the reception, help with clean up.

Shopping List

Number of guests	25	50	75
Italian Green Beans (15 oz. cans)	6	12	18
Sugar	1 cup	2 cups	3 cups
Vegetable oil	3 Tbsp.	6 Tbsp.	9 Tbsp.
Raw bacon strips, diced	2	4	6
Salt	2 tsp.	4 tsp.	2 Tbsp.
Pepper	1 tsp.	2 tsp.	3 tsp.
Large bowls	3	1	2
Serving spoons	2	4	6

Oughta-Be-Illegal Green Beans

Combine all ingredients in a large pot. Simmer covered on stove top for two hours. Cover with foil and refrigerate or serve immediately.

Team 6: Southern Style Pork and Beans Team

Helper #1 _____

Helper #2 _____

Reception Coordinator _____

Reception Location _____

Time of Ceremony _____

Number of Guests _____

Responsibilities

⚘ Make the beans early on the day of the wedding.

⚘ Arrive at the reception site no more than 30 minutes before the ceremony begins. Place the beans in the oven to keep warm. If no oven space is available, keep the foil-wrapped bowl in a cooler that has no ice in it—this will help the beans stay warm. Before the reception begins, place your bowl(s) of beans in their designated spots on the buffet table (see the Buffet Table diagram on page 116 for placement).

⚘ Keep your back-up beans in an oven on low heat or in an ice-free cooler. During the reception, keep an eye on your beans and if they begin to run low, replenish them.

⚘ At the end of the reception, help with clean up.

Shopping List

Number of guests	25	50	75
Pork and beans (15 oz. cans)	4	8	12
Light brown sugar	1 lb.	2 lbs.	3 lbs.
Medium onion, diced	1	2	3
Green pepper, diced	1	2	3
Raw bacon strips, diced	4	8	12
Baking dishes	1	2	3
Serving spoons	2	4	6

Southern Style Pork and Beans

Mix all ingredients together in a large mixing bowl. Pour into a large baking dish(es). Cover and bake at 325 degrees for 40 minutes or until bubbly hot.

Team 7: Mother Frye's Potato Salad Team

Helper #1 _____

Helper #2 _____

Reception Coordinator _____

Reception Location _____

Time of Ceremony _____

Number of Guests _____

Responsibilities

❧ Make the potato salad the day before the wedding and refrigerate overnight.

❧ Arrive at the reception site no more than 30 minutes before the ceremony. Place your bowls of potato salad in their designated spots on the buffet table (see the Buffet Table diagram on page 116 for placement).

❧ Keep your back-up potato salad (if any) in a refrigerator at the reception site. If no refrigerator is available, keep it in a cool place out of direct sunlight.

❧ During the reception, keep an eye on your potato salad and replenish it when it begins to run low.

❧ At the end of the reception, help with clean up.

Shopping List

Number of guests	25	50	75
Medium potatoes, diced	8 lbs.	16 lbs.	24 lbs.
Mayonnaise	4½ cups	9 cups	13½ cups
Sour cream	1½ cups	3 cups	4½ cups
Yellow mustard	1½ cups	3 cups	4½ cups
Fresh, chopped celery	3 cups	6 cups	9 cups
Fresh, chopped green onion	1½ cups	3 cups	4½ cups
Celery seed	3 Tbsp.	6 Tbsp.	9 Tbsp.
Salt	2 tsp.	4 tsp.	6 tsp.
Large bowls	1	2	3
Serving spoons	2	4	6

Mother Frye's Potato Salad

Prepare the potato salad a day ahead of time.

Peel potatoes and dice into ½" cubes. Boil diced potatoes until cooked but still firm (about 15 minutes). Drain and cool for about one hour.

In a large mixing bowl, whip together the mayonnaise, sour cream, mustard, celery seed, and salt. Fold in the celery and green onion.

Pour mixture over the cooled, diced potatoes and toss until well mixed. Do not overmix.

Cover with plastic wrap and refrigerate overnight.

Team 8: Carolina Coleslaw Team

Helper #1 _____

Helper #2 _____

Reception Coordinator _____

Reception Location _____

Time of Ceremony _____

Number of Guests _____

Responsibilities

- Make the coleslaw the day before the wedding and refrigerate overnight.

- Arrive at the reception site no more than 30 minutes before the ceremony. Place your bowls of coleslaw in their designated spots on the buffet table (see the Buffet Table diagram on page 116 for placement).

- Keep your back-up coleslaw (if any) in a refrigerator at the reception site. If no refrigerator is available, keep it in a cool place out of direct sunlight.

- During the reception, keep an eye on your coleslaw and replenish it when it begins to run low.

- At the end of the reception, help with clean up.

Shopping List

Number of guests	25	50	75
Cabbage, finely chopped	20 cups	32 cups	44 cups
(roughly equivalent to)	(2 heads)	(2–3 heads)	(4–5 heads)
Carrots, peeled and shredded	2 cups	4 cups	6 cups
(roughly equivalent to)	(4 carrots)	(8 carrots)	(12 carrots)
Green olives, chopped	1½ cups	3 cups	4½ cups
Onion, finely diced	¾ cup	1½ cups	2¼ cups
Caraway seed	1 Tbsp.	2 Tbsp.	3 Tbsp.
Sour cream	1½ cups	3 cups	4½ cups
Salt	1 Tbsp.	2 Tbsp.	3 Tbsp.
Sugar	1 tsp.	2 tsp.	3 tsp.
Vinegar	1/3 cup	2/3 cup	1 cup
Salad oil	3 Tbsp.	6 Tbsp.	½ cup
Pepper	½ tsp.	1 tsp.	1½ tsp.
Large bowls		1	2 3
Serving spoons	2	4	6

Carolina Coleslaw

In a large mixing bowl, whip together the sour cream, caraway seed, sugar, salt, pepper, oil, and vinegar. In a separate large bowl, mix together the cabbage, carrots, olives, and onion. Pour the liquid mixture into the cabbage mix and toss until well blended. Cover with plastic wrap and refrigerate until ready to serve.

Team 9: Yeast Rolls and Bread and Butter Pickles Team

Helper #1 _____

Reception Coordinator _____

Reception Location _____

Time of Ceremony _____

Number of Guests _____

Responsibilities

- For the best taste, bake the rolls so that they're ready right before it's time to leave for the ceremony.

- Arrive at the reception site no more than 15 minutes before the ceremony. Place the rolls and butter in their designated spots on the buffet table (see the Buffet Table diagram on page 116).

- Open the pickle jars and pour the pickles into bowls. Place the bowls and forks on the buffet table in their designated spots.

- Keep your back-up butter refrigerated or in a cool place out of direct sunlight. The back-up rolls should also be kept handy for replenishing. If there's an oven available, keep them warm until they're needed.

- At the end of the reception, help with clean up.

Shopping List

Number of guests	25	50	75
Bridgeford Parkerhouse Style Rolls (frozen dough, 24 ct.) OR Rich's Homestyle Roll Dough (24 ct.) or your favorite frozen roll dough	1½ pkgs.	3 pkgs.	4½ pkgs.
Butter (4 oz sticks)	3 sticks	6 sticks	9 sticks
Butter dish	2	3	5
Butter knives	2	3	5
Baskets	2	4	6
Bread and Butter Pickles (16 oz jars)	2	4	6
Bowls	2	2	4
Forks	4	4	8

Yeast Rolls

Follow directions on package for preparing rolls. Place hot rolls in baskets and cover with tin foil until ready to serve.

Team 10: Homemade Ice Cream Team

Helper #1 _____

Helper #2 _____

Reception Coordinator _____

Reception Location _____

Time of Ceremony _____

Number of Guests _____

Responsibilities

❧ Make the ice cream a day or two in advance. Because you'll have to keep it frozen for a few days, you might want to clean out your freezer ahead of time so you'll have plenty of room to store it.

❧ Arrive at the reception site no more than 15 minutes before the ceremony. Put two large serving spoons in their designated spots on the Wedding Cake Table (see the Wedding Cake Table diagram on page 116) but keep the ice cream in the freezer until immediately before the reception begins. If a freezer isn't available, put it in a cooler or a cool place out of direct sunlight. At the beginning of the reception, set the ice cream in its designated spot on the wedding cake table. Leave the back-up ice cream (if any) in the cooler or freezer until it's needed.

❧ Dip and serve the ice cream when the cake is served (another reception team member will cut and serve the cake).

❧ At the end of the reception, help with clean up.

Shopping List

Number of guests	25	50	75
	1 gallon	**2 gallons**	**3 gallons**
Whole milk	5 cups	10 cups	15 cups
Sugar	2¼ cups	4½ cups	6 ¾ cups
All-purpose flour	¼ cup + 2 Tbsp.	¾ cup	1 cup + 1 Tbsp.
Salt	¼ tsp.	½ tsp.	¾ tsp.
Eggs (beaten)	5	10	15
Haf-and-half	1 qt.	2 qts.	3 qts.
Vanilla extract	1½ Tbsp.	3 Tbsp.	4½ Tbsp.
Yield	32 servings	64 servings	96 servings
6 qt. ice cream maker	1	*2	*3
Serving spoon	1	2	3

Note: To avoid having to round up several ice cream makers, start a day or two prior to the reception and make several batches in one ice cream maker. Store the ice cream in plastic one-gallon bowls or containers in the freezer. Remember, the ice cream will be served out of whatever you freeze it in, so make sure your containers look nice.

Homemade Ice Cream

In a saucepan, heat milk until hot (do not boil).

Mix together the sugar, flour, and salt. Slowly add this dry mixture to the hot milk and stir well. Cook mixture over medium heat, stirring constantly, for 15 minutes or until it has thickened.

Break eggs into a medium-sized bowl and stir with a fork, breaking yolks.

Slowly add ¼ of hot mixture to the eggs and stir. When mixed together well, add the egg mixture to the remaining hot milk-and-sugar mixture in the saucepan, stirring constantly. Cook for 1 minute, remove from heat, and let cool. Chill for 2 ½ hours.

In a large bowl, combine the half-and-half and vanilla. Add the chilled custard and whip well. Pour the mixture into the ice cream can.

Follow the ice cream maker's instructions for freezing the ice cream. When ice cream is ready, remove can from ice cream maker, transfer the ice cream to a serving container, and place in the freezer.

Team 11: Iced Tea and Coffee Team

Helper #1 _____

Helper #2 _____

Reception Coordinator _____

Reception Location _____

Time of Ceremony _____

Number of Guests _____

Responsibilities

- Make small signs for regular and decaffeinated coffee.

- Make the tea no more than six hours before the reception begins. If you make it earlier than that, the tea will sour.

- Stop by a convenience store on the way to the wedding and buy ice. Break the bags open into your clean ice chests and place an ice scoop in each cooler.

- The coffee will take 30 minutes to an hour to brew. Arrive at the reception site in plenty of time for the coffee to be ready by the beginning of the reception. The coffee urn(s) will be waiting for you at the reception site.

- Pour iced tea into the drink dispenser that will be waiting for you at the reception site.

- Using the Drink Station diagram on page 117, arrange the cups, saucers, creamer, and bowls of sugar, sweetener, and lemon wedges on the beverage table. Place the coffee signs/placards in front of the appropriate coffee urn. Back-up supplies can go under the table.

- Ten minutes before the reception begins, fill all your glasses with ice and tea so guests won't have to wait in line to fill their own and traffic around the beverage table will be kept to a minimum.

- After everyone has gotten their tea, refill the dispenser and place the coolers near the tea so that guests may refill their own glasses. Be sure the ice scoop is visible for them to use.

- During the reception, keep an eye on the table and replenish sugar, creamer, and so forth if necessary.

- At the end of the reception, help with clean up.

Shopping List

Number of guests	25	50	75
For Sweetened Ice Tea			
Plastic 1-gallon container	3	6	9
Luzianne family-size tea bags or your favorite brand tea bag	15	30	45
Water	3 gallons	6 gallons	9 gallons
Sugar	9 cups	18 cups	27 cups
Lemons	4	8	12
Glass bowls	2	2	2
Forks	2	2	2
Ice chest	2	2	2
Ice scoop	2	2	2
10- to 12-cup coffeemaker	1	1	1
Ice	15 lbs.	30 lbs.	45 lbs.
For Coffee			
Regular coffee	5 oz	10 oz	15 oz
Decaffeinated coffee	5 oz	10 oz	15 oz
Water	25 cups	50 cups	75 cups
Sugar	¼ lb.	½ lb.	¾ lb.
Sweet 'N Low (Packets)	12	24	36
Equal (Packets)	10	20	30
Cream (half-and-half)	½ qt.	1 qt.	1½ qts.
Glass bowls	6	6	6
"Regular" sign	1	1	1
"Decaffeinated" sign	1	1	1
12' 3-pronged extension cords	2	2	2

Sweetened Iced Tea

Note: This recipe makes one gallon of iced tea. For 25 guests, make three batches. For 50 guests, make six batches. For 75 guests, make nine batches. Don't make the tea more than six hours before the reception or it will sour.

Fill your coffee pot full of water and brew 5 tea bags. Pour the hot tea into a 1-gallon container and add warm water until it's full.

Add sugar and stir well until it dissolves. Put the lid on the container and refrigerate.

Cut lemons into eighths and place them into two bowls. Cover with plastic wrap and refrigerate. (If the lemon wedges won't all fit in the bowls, put the extras in a plastic baggie and use them to replenish the bowls during the reception.)

Regular and Decaffeinated Coffee

Make the coffee at the reception site.

Remove the lids, filters, and stems from the coffee pots. Fill the pots to the correct water line (look for lines inside the pots). Reinsert the stems and filters. Fill the filters with the desired amount of coffee (read the labels on the coffee can to find out how much coffee to measure into the filters). Secure the lids and turn the coffee urns on. The coffee will take from 30 minutes to an hour to brew.

Backyard Barbecue
Reception for 25 Guests

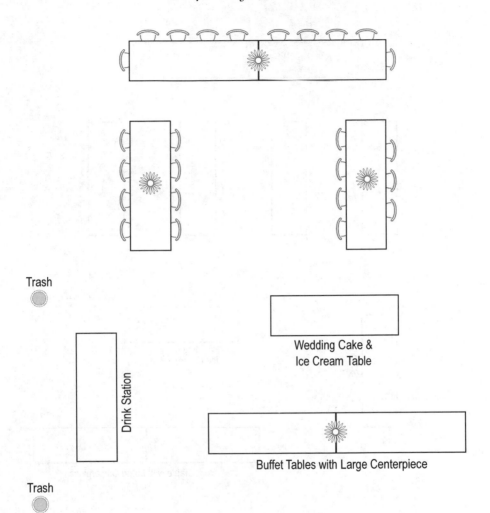

Trash

Wedding Cake &
Ice Cream Table

Drink Station

Buffet Tables with Large Centerpiece

Trash

Backyard Barbecue
Reception for 50 Guests

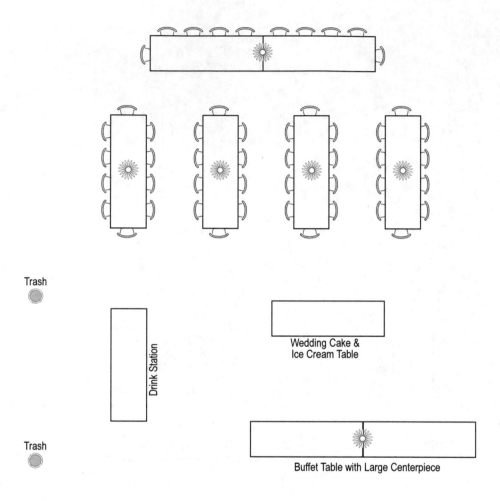

Trash

Drink Station

Wedding Cake &
Ice Cream Table

Buffet Table with Large Centerpiece

Backyard Barbecue
Reception for 75 Guests

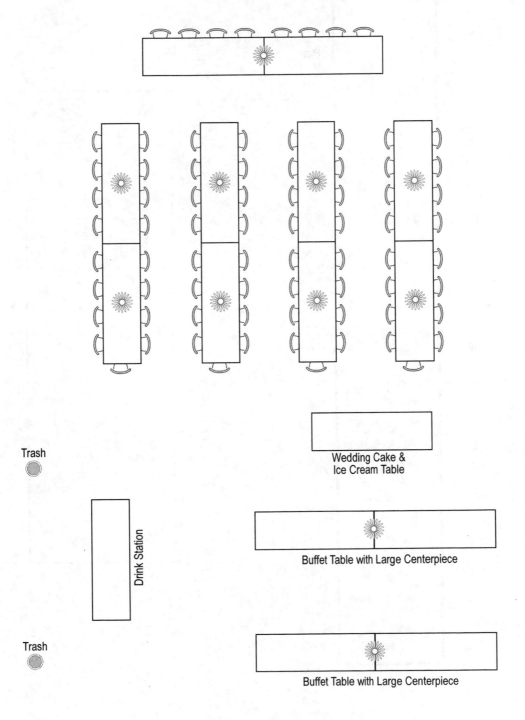

Trash

Wedding Cake &
Ice Cream Table

Drink Station

Buffet Table with Large Centerpiece

Trash

Buffet Table with Large Centerpiece

Backyard Barbecue Reception Buffet Table

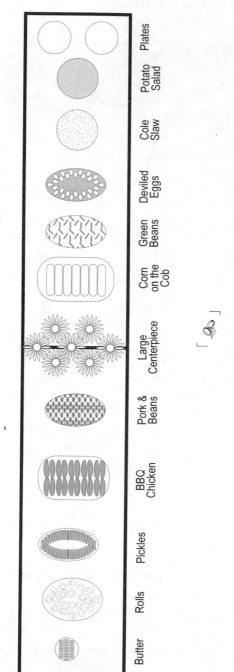

Butter — Rolls — Pickles — BBQ Chicken — Pork & Beans — Large Centerpiece — Corn on the Cob — Green Beans — Deviled Eggs — Cole Slaw — Potato Salad — Plates

Backyard Barbecue Reception Wedding Cake and Ice Cream Table

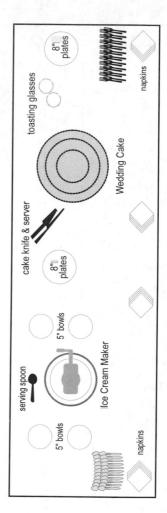

Backyard Barbecue Reception
Drink Station

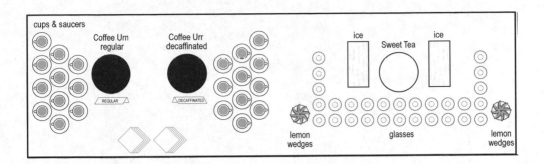

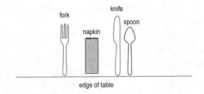

Backyard Barbecue Reception
Place Setting

 *Chapter 6*

The Brunch Reception

Mid-morning weddings with brunch receptions are gaining in popularity, especially among couples who don't have a burning desire to dance their wedding night away. It may be hard to believe, but not all couples need the Chicken Dance and the Hokey Pokey to adequately express the emotions and sentiment they feel on their wedding day.

This plan offers simple but elegant dishes for more intimate-sized receptions—25 to 75 people. If you fall in love with the idea of a brunch reception but you've got a larger guest list, you can easily increase the recipes to accommodate bigger crowds. To pull it off, though, you'll need to find more people who'd be willing to help you or ask the ones who've already signed on to your team to prepare greater volumes of food. For the Rice Pilaf with Toasted Almonds and the Chicken and Green Bean Casserole teams, this will mean cooking and freezing in batches ahead of time because not many home kitchens have the equipment to prepare huge quantities of these dishes in one sitting.

Depending on the number of guests you're inviting, you'll need 13 to 17 reliable friends to help you pull the Brunch Reception together. Because yours will be a morning wedding, find some early risers for jobs like setting up the reception hall and cooking some of the menu items. Most of your helpers, though, can make their items a day ahead of time and hug the mattress until it's time to get ready for the ceremony.

The Menu

Layered Vegetable Salad
Fruit Salad a la Orange
Chicken and Green Bean Casserole
Rice Pilaf with Toasted Almonds
Roast Beef Pocket Sandwiches
Cranberry Relish
Sweet Potato Biscuits
Regular and Decaffeinated Coffee
Champagne Punch

The Helpers

You'll need 10 teams—13 to 17 people—to help with this reception. Detailed job descriptions for each team are provided later in this chapter, but here's a quick summary of the type of help you're looking for.

Setup/Take-Down Team: You know your muscle-bound buddies who like to practice their professional wrestling moves? These are the guys you want for this job! You'll need two people to set up the hall for the reception then take everything down when it's over. You may want to ask another friend with a sense of style to help on this team, which is also responsible for laying out tablecloths and decorations and making the place look nice.

Layered Vegetable Salad Team: Boiling water and frying bacon are as close as this team comes to actual cooking, so you don't have to look for a culinary genius for this one.

Fruit Salad a la Orange Team: Call this one-person team "Slicers and Dicers R Us!" The only requirement, aside from the ability to handle a knife without doing bodily harm to bystanders, is a refrigerator with a lot of space.

Chicken and Green Bean Casserole Team: This is a job for a couple of people who have two things: time to make several batches of casseroles and freezer space to store it all in. Instead of working together to make the casseroles, this team's members will probably want to divide up the number of required batches among them and make them in their own kitchens.

Rice Pilaf with Toasted Almonds Team: If you have a large guest list, this is another one that will need to be divided between two team members and cooked up in separate kitchens. The recipe's not difficult, but the team will need a lot of stove top and oven space.

Roast Beef Pocket Sandwiches Team: What could be easier than stuffing pita bread halves? This team of two can make this recipe with their eyes closed.

Cranberry Relish Team: Actually, there *is* one job that's easier than stuffing pita bread halves—this one! This team of one person also has the honor of cutting and serving the wedding cake.

Sweet Potato Biscuits Team: Although this isn't a very difficult recipe, recruit someone with a little baking experience for this job. This team also gets to cut and serve the groom's cake if one is provided.

Coffee Team: If they can fill a pot with water, they're qualified to be the official caretakers of the reception coffee urn. This team requires only one or two people.

Champagne Punch Team: This job is a little more complicated than the coffee job, but that's not saying much! Recruit one or two people for this assignment.

The Hardware

In addition to recruiting the people who will help you with your reception, you'll need to get your hands on the items listed here. Before heading to the rental store and whipping out your credit card, however, read Chapter 9 for complete information on renting and otherwise acquiring the supplies you'll need for your reception.

Included in this list are white table linens, centerpieces, and floral arrangements. These are staples at traditional wedding receptions, but you may want to use some other type of decorations. Chapter 8 covers decorating your reception site and has some unique and out-of-the-ordinary decorating ideas you may want to consider.

Number of guests	25	50	75
8' x 30" banquet tables	8	6	15
54" x 120" white tablecloths	8	6	15
21' white skirting segments	4	5	7
60" round tables	0	5	1
120" white round tablecloths	0	5	1
White Samsonite chairs	25	50	75
12" white china dinner plates	25	50	75
Dinner forks	25	50	75
Dinner knives	25	50	75
Dinner spoons	25	50	75
5-oz glass punch cups	25	50	75
20" x 20" white linen napkins	25	50	75
White coffee cups	25	50	75
White coffee saucers	25	50	75
Salt and pepper shakers	4 sets	7 sets	9 sets
Glass sugar bowls	8	14	18
Glass creamers	4	7	9
11-qt. glass punch bowl and ladle	1 set	1 set	1 set
Coffee urns	2-25 cup	2-50 cup	2-90 cup
Floral centerpiece for buffet	1	1	2
Floral centerpieces for guest tables	3	6	8
8" glass plates	25	50	75
Cake knife and server	1 set	1 set	1 set
Wedding cake	1	1	1
Engraved cocktail napkins	65	125	200
Toasting glasses	1 set	1 set	1 set

*Note: Have your rentals delivered the day **before** the reception. You don't want your setup team waiting around for a delivery. All items should be there when the team arrives so that they can immediately start setting up.*

Reception Team Job Descriptions

Team 1: Setup/Take-Down Team

Helper #1 _____

Helper #2 _____

Helper #3 _____

Reception Coordinator _____

Reception Location _____

Time of Ceremony _____

Number of Guests _____

Responsibilities

❧ Clean out two large plastic trash cans for use at the reception. Because these will be seen by guests, try to find cans that are presentable. Be sure to bring about a half dozen trash can liners.

❧ Arrive at the reception site about four hours before the ceremony to arrange tables and chairs in their designated locations (see the Brunch Reception Room diagrams on pages 140 to 142).

❧ Place tablecloths and skirting on tables as follows:

- **For 25 guests:** Four 8' x 30" tables (wedding cake, drink station, and buffet tables) and 54" x 120" tablecloths. Clip skirting on *before* laying the tablecloth on the table. Four 8' x 30" tables (guest tables) and 54" x 120" tablecloths—no skirting required.

- **For 50 guests:** Four 8' x 30" tables (wedding cake, drink station, and buffet tables) and 54" x 120" tablecloths. Clip skirting on *before* laying the tablecloth on the table. Five 60" round tables (120" round tablecloths) and two 8' x 30" tables (54" x 120" tablecloths) for guests—no skirting required.

- **For 75 guests:** Seven 8' x 30" tables (wedding cake, drink station, and buffet tables) and 54" x 120" tablecloths. Clip skirting on *before* laying the tablecloth on the table. One 60" round table (120" round tablecloth) and eight 8' x 30" tables (54" x 120" tablecloths) for guests—no skirting required.

❧ If more than one color will be used on the tables, the bride will let you know how the linens should be arranged.

- The bride will provide items such as dishes, silverware, the punch bowl, and centerpieces and have them delivered to the reception site. Using the diagrams for the Buffet Table, Wedding Cake Table, Reception Drink Station (see pages 143 and 144), arrange the items on the appropriate tables.

- During the reception, help keep the area neat and clean. Keep an eye on the trash cans and change the liners when they get full.

- At the end of the reception, help with clean up and return all the rented items to the location of the room where they were delivered.

Team 2: Layered Vegetable Salad Team

Helper #1: _____

Reception Coordinator _____

Reception Location _____

Time of Ceremony _____

Number of Guests _____

Responsibilities

- The day before the reception, make Layered Vegetable Salad according to the recipe on page 125. Because the salad needs to be refrigerated, you might want to clean out your fridge ahead of time so you'll have plenty of room to store it.

- Arrive at the reception site no more than 30 minutes before the ceremony and place the bowls of salad on the buffet tables as shown on the Buffet Table diagram on page 143. The extra salad should be refrigerated at the reception site. If no refrigerator is available, store it in a shady, cool spot out of direct sunlight.

- Keep an eye on your bowls during the reception and replenish them when necessary.

- At the end of the reception, help with clean up.

Shopping List

Number of guests	25	50	75
Shredded iceberg lettuce (roughly equivalent to)	18 cups (2 heads)	36 cups (3–4 heads)	54 cups (5–6 heads)
Salt and pepper	to taste	to taste	to taste
Sugar	2 tsp.	4 tsp.	2 Tbsp.
Hard-boiled eggs, sliced	18	36	54
10 oz. frozen English peas, thawed	3 packs	6 packs	9 packs
Bacon, cooked and crumbled	3 lbs.	6 lbs.	9 lbs.
Swiss cheese, shredded	6 cups	12 cups	18 cups
Mayonnaise, cold	3 cups	6 cups	2¼ qts.
Green onions (fresh, diced)	1 cup	2 cups	3 cups
Paprika	sprinkle	sprinkle	sprinkle
3-qt. casserole dish	2	4	6
Large serving spoons	2	4	6

Layered Vegetable Salad

Divide half of the lettuce among your glass casserole dishes and place inside. Sprinkle with salt, pepper, and sugar.

Layer sliced eggs over the top of the lettuce. Sprinkle with salt.

Layer the peas over the top of the eggs.

Layer remaining lettuce over the top of the peas.

Layer bacon and then cheese over lettuce.

Spread the mayonnaise over the entire top of salad, going all the way to the edges.

Cover tightly with plastic wrap and refrigerate for 24 hours.

Right before serving, sprinkle the green onions and paprika on top of the salad.

Team 3: Fruit Salad a la Orange Team

Helper #1 _____

Reception Coordinator _____

Reception Location _____

Time of Ceremony _____

Number of Guests _____

Responsibilities

❧ The day before the reception, make the fruit salad cups according to the recipe on page 127. Because the fruit salad cups need to be refrigerated, you might want to clean out your fridge ahead of time so you'll have plenty of room to store them.

❧ Arrive at the reception site no more than 30 minutes before the ceremony and place the tongs and trays of fruit salad cups on the buffet tables as shown on the Buffet Table diagram on page 143. Your extra cups should be refrigerated at the reception site. If no refrigerator is available, store them in a shady, cool spot out of direct sunlight.

❧ Keep an eye on your trays during the reception and replenish them when necessary.

❧ At the end of the reception, help with clean up.

Shopping List

Number of guests	25	50	75
Fresh medium-sized oranges	13	25	38
Fresh bananas, cut in half and sliced	2	4	6
Apples, peeled and diced	2	4	6
Miniature marshmallows	2 cups	4 cups	6 cups
Green grapes, seedless and halved	½ cup	1 cup	1½ cups
Red grapes, seedless and halved	½ cup	1 cup	1½ cups
Sour cream, divided	1 lb.	2 lbs.	3 lbs.
Honey	¼ cup	½ cup	¾ cup
Salt	½ tsp.	1 tsp.	1½ tsp.
20" serving trays	1	1	2
Tongs	2	2	4

Fruit Salad a la Orange

Cut oranges in half crosswise. Remove the pulp from the orange halves with a spoon and reserve. Set the cups off to the side. Dice the orange pulp and drain well, being careful to remove all of the seeds.

Combine the orange pulp, bananas, apples, marshmallows, and grapes. Reserve a portion of the red grapes as these will be used for garnishing the tops of the cups.

Combine half of the sour cream with the honey and mix well. Cover and refrigerate; you'll use this tomorrow to garnish the orange cups.

Add the salt to the remaining sour cream, mixing well. Pour the sour cream-and-salt mixture into the fruit and toss gently.

Stuff each cup with the fruit salad. Arrange orange cups on your trays, cover with plastic wrap, and refrigerate. Place extras on cookie sheets, cover and refrigerate; you'll use these to replenish the trays during the reception.

Shortly before leaving for the reception, place a spoonful of the honey/sour cream mixture and half a red grape on top of each orange cup. Cover loosely with plastic wrap and refrigerate.

Team 4: Chicken and Green Bean Casserole Team

Helper #1 _____

Helper #2 _____

Reception Coordinator _____

Reception Location _____

Time of Ceremony _____

Number of Guests _____

Responsibilities

- Make the casseroles the day before the reception. (You can make them up to a month before and freeze them if you'd like.) Be sure to allow enough time to reheat them thoroughly before the reception. Wrap the hot casseroles in foil to keep them warm.

❧ Arrive at the reception site no more than 30 minutes before the ceremony and place the casseroles in the oven to keep warm. If no oven space is available, keep them in a cooler that has no ice in it—this will help them stay warm. Before the reception begins, place the casseroles and serving spoons on the buffet tables as shown on the Buffet Table diagram on page 143. Keep your extra casseroles in the oven or cooler to keep them warm.

❧ Keep an eye on your casseroles during the reception and replenish them when necessary.

❧ At the end of the reception, help with clean up.

Shopping List

Number of guests	25	50	75
Whole 3-lb. chicken, cut up	4	8	12
Celery, chopped	1 cup	2 cups	3 cups
Carrot, chopped	1 cup	2 cups	3 cups
Onion, chopped	2 cups	4 cups	6 cups
Herb stuffing mix, divided	8 cups	16 cups	24 cups
French-style green beans (drained 16 oz can)	4	8	12
Fresh mushrooms, chopped	2 cups	4 cups	6 cups
Cashews, chopped	1 cup	2 cups	3 cups
Cream of mushroom soup (undiluted 10 ¾ oz can)	4	8	12
Milk	2 cups	4 cups	6 cups
Melted margarine	½ cup	1 cup	1½ cups
Chicken stock (from cooking chicken)	5 cups	10 cups	15 cups
Yield,	28 servings	56 servings	84 servings
12" x 8" x 2" baking dish	4	8	12

Chicken and Green Bean Casserole

Note: This recipe makes one batch of Chicken and Green Bean Casserole—most home kitchens don't have large enough pots or adequate oven space to cook more than one or two batches at a time. For 25 guests, make four batches. For 50 guests, make eight batches. For 75 guests, make 12 batches. A single batch makes eight servings.

Single batch of Chicken and Green Bean Casserole

1 3-lb. chicken
1/4 cup shopped carrots
2 cups stuffing mix
1/2 cup chopped
   fresh mushrooms
1 10 3/4oz can cream of
   mushroom soup (undiluted)
1/2 cup milk
1 12" x 8" x 2" baking dish

1/4 cup chopped celery
1/4 cup chopped onion
1 16 oz. can French-style
   green beans (drained)
1/4 cup chopped cashews
1 1/4 cups chicken stock
   (from cooking chicken)
2 Tbsp. butter or margarine (melted)

Place chicken, celery, carrots, and onions in a large pot and cover with cold water. Bring to a boil, then reduce heat and simmer for one hour.

Remove the chicken and allow to cool. Set the pot of stock aside for later use. Remove all the chicken meat from the bone and cut into ½" pieces. Set aside.

Pour half of the stuffing mix into your lightly greased 12" x 8" x 2" baking dishes. Layer the green beans, mushrooms, cashews, and chicken over the stuffing.

Mix the mushroom soup, milk and 3/4 cup of chicken broth together and pour over the top of the chicken.

Combine the other half of stuffing mix with 1/2 cup of the reserved chicken stock and the margarine. Sprinkle on top of the soup mixture.

Bake uncovered at 350 degrees for 30 minutes or until bubbly.

You may make the casseroles up to a month early and freeze them using the following method. Bake the casseroles then allow them to cool for 30 minutes. Cover the casseroles with plastic wrap then with foil. Using a toothpick, poke several holes through the foil and plastic wrap and refrigerate for two hours before moving to the freezer. To reheat, remove from the freezer to thaw in the refrigerator 24 hours before the wedding. Once thawed, remove the foil and plastic wrap and bake uncovered in a 350 degree oven for 30 minutes or until bubbly.

Team 5: Rice Pilaf with Toasted Almonds Team

Helper #1 _____

Helper #2 _____

Reception Coordinator _____

Reception Location _____

Time of Ceremony _____

Number of Guests _____

Responsibilities

☙ Make the pilafs the day before the reception. (You can make them up to a month before and freeze them if you'd like.) Be sure to allow enough time to reheat them thoroughly before the reception. Wrap the hot pilafs in foil to keep them warm.

☙ Arrive at the reception site no more than 30 minutes before the ceremony and place the pilafs in the oven to keep warm. If no oven space is available, keep them in a cooler that has no ice in it. Before the reception begins, place the pilafs and serving spoons on the buffet tables as shown on the Buffet Table diagram on page 143. Keep your extra pilafs warm in the oven or cooler.

☙ Keep the rice pilaf replenished during the reception.

☙ At the end of the reception, help with clean up.

Shopping List

Number of guests	25	50	75
Onion, chopped	2½ cups	5 cups	7½ cups
Butter or margarine, melted	1¼ cups	2½ cups	3¾ cups
Uncooked long-grain rice	5 cups	10 cups	15 cups
Raisins, divided	1¼ cups	2½ cups	3¾ cups
Water	2½ qts.	5 qts.	7½ qts.
Chicken-flavored bouillon cubes	10	20	30
Salt	¾ tsp.	1½ tsp.	2¼ tsp.
Pepper	¾ tsp.	1½ tsp.	2¼ tsp.
Ground thyme	¼ tsp.	½ tsp.	¾ tsp.
Ground oregano	¼ tsp.	½ tsp.	¾ tsp.
Slivered almonds, toasted and divided	1¾ cups	3½ cups	5¼ cups
Salted peanuts, divided	1¾ cups	3½ cups	5¼ cups
3-qt. casserole dishes	2	4	6
Serving spoons	4	8	12

Rice Pilaf with Toasted Almonds

Note: This recipe makes one batch of Rice Pilaf with Toasted Almonds—most home kitchens don't have large enough pots or adequate oven space to cook more than one or two batches at a time. For 25 guests, make four batches. For 50 guests, make eight batches. For 75 guests, make 12 batches. A single batch makes six servings.

Single batch of Rice Pilaf with Toasted Almonds

1/2 cup onion, chopped	1/4 cup butter or margarine, melted
1 cup uncooked long-grain rice	1/4 cup raisins, divided in half
2 cups water	2 chicken flavored bouillon cubes
1/8 tsp. salt	1/8 tsp. pepper
Pinch of ground thyme	Pinch of ground oregano
1/4 cup peanuts, divided	1/4 cup slivered almonds, toasted
1 1 1/2 qt. baking dish per batch	and divided

Sauté onion with butter in a saucepot until onion is transparent. Add rice and cook over low heat until rice is slightly browned. Stir frequently. Remove from heat and stir in half of the raisins, peanuts, and almonds. Lightly grease your casserole dishes and divide the rice mixture equally among them.

In a saucepan, combine water and bouillon cubes and bring to a boil. Add salt, pepper, thyme, and oregano. Divide this mixture equally among casserole dishes and pour over the rice. Cover and bake at 350 degrees for 30 minutes or until rice is tender. Garnish with the remaining peanuts, toasted almonds, and raisins.

You may make the pilafs up to a month early and freeze them using the following method. Bake the pilafs then allow them to cool for 30 minutes. Cover the pilafs with plastic wrap then with foil. Using a toothpick, poke several holes through the foil and plastic wrap and refrigerate for two hours before moving to the freezer. To reheat, remove from the freezer to thaw in the refrigerator 24 hours before the wedding. Once thawed, remove the foil and plastic wrap and bake uncovered in a 350 degree oven for 30 minutes.

Note: To toast almonds, spread the almonds out on a cookie sheet. Bake at 350 degrees for 5-8 minutes or until lightly browned.

Team 6: Roast Beef Pocket Sandwiches Team

Helper #1 _____

Helper #2 _____

Reception Coordinator _____

Reception Location _____

Time of Ceremony _____

Number of Guests _____

Responsibilities

❧ The day before or early on the day of the reception, make the sandwiches according to the recipe on page 133. Because the sandwiches need to be refrigerated, you might want to clean out your fridge ahead of time so you'll have plenty of room to store them.

❧ Arrive at the reception site no more than 30 minutes before the ceremony and place the trays of sandwiches and tongs on the buffet tables as shown on the Buffet Table diagram on page 143. Your extra sandwiches should be refrigerated at the reception site. If no refrigerator is available, store them in a shady, cool spot out of direct sunlight.

❧ Keep your trays replenished during the reception.

❧ At the end of the reception, help with clean up.

Shopping List

Number of guests	25	50	75
Romaine lettuce, shredded	6¼ cups	12½ cups	19 cups
(roughly equivalent to)	(1–2 heads)	(2–3 heads)	(4–5 heads)
Fresh spinach, shredded	2½ cups	5 cups	7½ cups
Greek olives, pitted and sliced	30	60	90
Fresh green onions, chopped	5	10	15
Radishes, sliced	5	10	15
Italian dressing	1 cup	2 cups	3 cups
Cream cheese, softened	1 lb.	2 lbs.	3 lbs.
6" pita bread, cut in half	13	25	38
Roast beef, chopped	2 lbs.	4 lbs.	6 lbs.
Yield	26	50	76
30" round tray	1	2	2
Serving tongs	2	4	4

Roast Beef Pocket Sandwiches

Mix the first six ingredients and toss gently. Let stand for 10 minutes.

Spread a layer of cream cheese on both inner sides of the pita pocket. Stuff each pocket with equal parts of roast beef and salad mixture.

Arrange prepared sandwiches on your trays. If you have extras, place them on cookies sheets; you'll use these to replenish the trays during the reception.

Cover tightly with plastic wrap and refrigerate.

Team 7: Cranberry Relish Team

Helper #1 _____

Reception Coordinator _____

Reception Location _____

Time of Ceremony _____

Number of Guests _____

Responsibilities

- The day before the reception, make the relish according to the recipe on page 134. Because the relish needs to be refrigerated, you might want to clean out your fridge ahead of time so you'll have plenty of room to store it.

- Arrive at the reception site no more than 30 minutes before the ceremony and place the bowls of relish on the buffet tables as shown on the Buffet Table diagram on page 143. The extra relish should be refrigerated at the reception site. If no refrigerator is available, store it in a shady, cool spot out of direct sunlight.

- Keep an eye on your bowls during the reception and replenish them when necessary.

- Help cut and serve wedding cake.

- At the end of the reception, help with clean up.

Shopping List

Number of guests	25	50	75
Fresh cranberries	2 cups	4 cups	6 cups
Fresh oranges, unpeeled	1	2	3
Sugar	2/3 cup	1 1/3 cup	2 cups
Boiling water	3½ cups	7 cups	10½ cups
Cherry-flavored gelatin, 3 oz pack	2	4	6
Medium-sized glass bowls	2	4	6
Serving spoons	2	4	6

Cranberry Relish

Wash and drain the cranberries.

Cut orange(s) into quarters, leaving the peel on.

Grind the cranberries and oranges together in a food processor on high for 45 seconds. Stir in the sugar.

In a separate bowl, add boiling water to gelatin and stir until dissolved. Cool for 20 minutes.

Stir in cranberry/orange mixture, pour into glass bowls, cover with plastic wrap, and refrigerate. If you have extra relish, put it into a spare bowl, cover with plastic wrap, and refrigerate. You'll use this to replenish your relish at the reception.

Team 8: Sweet Potato Biscuits Team

Helper #1 _____

Reception Coordinator _____

Reception Location _____

Time of Ceremony _____

Number of Guests _____

Responsibilities

⁓ Make the biscuits early on the day of the reception. Wrap the hot biscuits in foil to keep them warm.

⁓ Arrive at the reception site no more than 30 minutes before the ceremony and place the baskets of biscuits on the buffet tables as shown on the Buffet Table diagram on page 143. Place your extra biscuits in a warm oven at the reception site. If no oven is available, bring a cooler with no ice and place the biscuits in it to keep them warm.

⁓ Keep an eye on the biscuits during the reception and replenish them when necessary.

⁓ Help cut and serve the groom's cake if one is provided.

⁓ At the end of the reception, help with clean up.

Shopping List

Number of guests	25	50	75
All-purpose flour	3 cups	6 cups	9 cups
Baking powder	4½ tsp.	3 Tbsp.	4½ Tbsp.
Salt	¾ tsp.	1½ tsp.	2¼ tsp.
Ground nutmeg	1/8 tsp.	¼ tsp.	3/8 tsp.
Mashed sweet potatoes, cooked	1½ cups	3 cups	4½ cups
Milk	1 cup	2 cups	3 cups
Vegetable oil	½ cup	1 cup	1½ cup
Yield, number of biscuits	30	60	90
Large bread basket(s)	1	2	2
Serving tongs	2	4	4
Butter (4 oz. sticks)	3 sticks	6 sticks	9 sticks
Butter dishes	2	3	5
Butter knives	2	3	5

Sweet Potato Biscuits

Combine the flour, baking powder, salt, and ground nutmeg. Mix well. Set aside.

Combine the remaining ingredients and pour into flour mixture. Stir until flour mixture is moistened. Flip dough out onto a heavily floured countertop and knead five times. You may need to add a little flour as you go. (This dough is very wet to work with, so keep your hands well floured as you knead it.) Roll out dough to ½" thick. Cut with a 2" cookie cutter.

Place biscuits on a lightly greased cookie sheet.

Bake at 425 degrees for 15 minutes or until lightly browned.

Team 9: Coffee Team

Helper #1 _____

Helper #2 _____

Reception Coordinator _____

Reception Location _____

Time of Ceremony _____

Number of Guests _____

Responsibilities

- Make small placards or signs for regular and decaffeinated coffee. You may want to make these on your computer or write them using calligraphy.

- The coffee will take 30 minutes to an hour to brew. Arrive at the reception site in plenty of time for the coffee to be ready by the beginning of the reception. The coffee urns will be waiting for you at the reception site.

- Fill half of the bowls with sugar, the other half with packets of artificial sweeteners. Fill the creamers with half-and-half. Place one sugar bowl, sweetener bowl, and creamer on each guest table. Place back-up supplies under the Drink Station table.

- At the end of the reception, help with clean up.

Shopping List

Number of guests	25	50	75
Regular coffee	5 oz.	10 oz.	15 oz.
Decaffeinated coffee	5 oz.	10 oz.	15 oz.
Water per urn	25 cups	50 cups	75 cups
Sugar	1 lb.	1½ lbs.	2 lbs.
Sweet 'N Low (packets)	50	75	100
Equal (packets)	25	35	50
Cream (half-and-half)	2 qts.	3 qts.	4 qts.
Glass bowls (softball size)	6	6	6
Regular sign	1	1	1
Decaffeinated sign	1	1	1
12' three-pronged extension cords	2	2	2

Coffee

At the reception site, make sure that the coffee table is located near electrical outlets. You may have to move the table closer to an outlet if you don't have easy access. Use your extension cords if necessary.

Remove the lids, filters, and stems from the coffee urns. Fill the pots to the correct water line (look for lines inside the pots). Reinsert the stems and filters. Fill the filters with the desired amount of coffee (read the labels on the coffee can to find out how much coffee to measure into the filters). Secure the lids and turn the coffee urns on. The coffee will take from 30 minutes to an hour to brew.

Team 10: Champagne Punch Team

Helper #1 _____

Helper #2 _____

Reception Coordinator _____

Reception Location _____

Time of Ceremony _____

Number of Guests _____

Responsibilities

❧ Gather all ingredients for the punch and arrive at the reception site one hour before the wedding. Decide ahead of time where you're going to get the ice and pick it up on your way to the reception site. Make the punch at the reception site according to the recipe on page 139.

❧ Fill the punch bowl with punch and keep it replenished during the reception. The bowl will be waiting for you at the hall.

❧ At the end of the reception, help with clean up.

Shopping List

Number of guests	25	50	75
Orange juice, chilled	3 qts.	6 qts.	9 qts.
Grapefruit juice, chilled	3 cups	6 cups	9 cups
Lemon juice, chilled	1½ cups	3 cups	4½ cups
Lime juice, chilled	1½ cups	3 cups	4½ cups
Almond extract	¼ oz	½ oz	¾ oz
Champagne, chilled, 25.4 oz bottle	6	12	18
Yield	2¼ gal.	4½ gal.	6¾ gal.
5-gallon buckets	1	1	2
1-gallon buckets	2	2	2
Cubed ice	15 lbs.	30 lbs.	45 lbs.
Medium-sized ice chests	1	2	3

Champagne Punch

In the 5-gallon buckets, combine first five ingredients (divided equally among the buckets).

Just before the reception, add champagne to the mix.

Because the 5-gallon buckets will be too heavy and cumbersome to lift easily, fill the 1-gallon buckets with punch and pour into the punch bowl. (The bowl will be waiting for you at the reception site.) Use the smaller buckets to refill the bowl during the reception. Store buckets of punch under the table.

Always add the ice directly to the punch bowl, not to the 1- or 5-gallon buckets. Store ice (in an ice chest) under the table.

Brunch Reception for 25 Guests

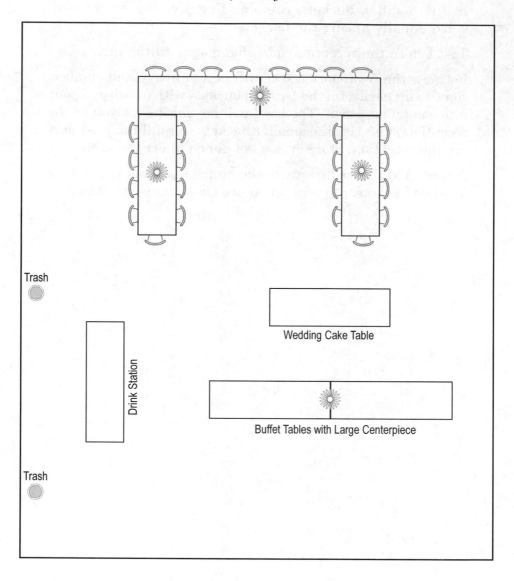

Trash

Wedding Cake Table

Drink Station

Buffet Tables with Large Centerpiece

Trash

Brunch Reception for 50 Guests

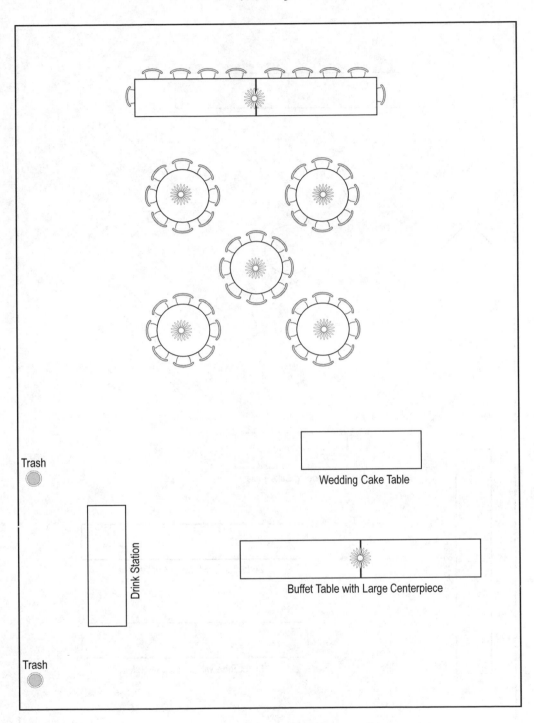

Wedding Cake Table

Drink Station

Trash

Trash

Buffet Table with Large Centerpiece

Brunch Reception for 75 Guests

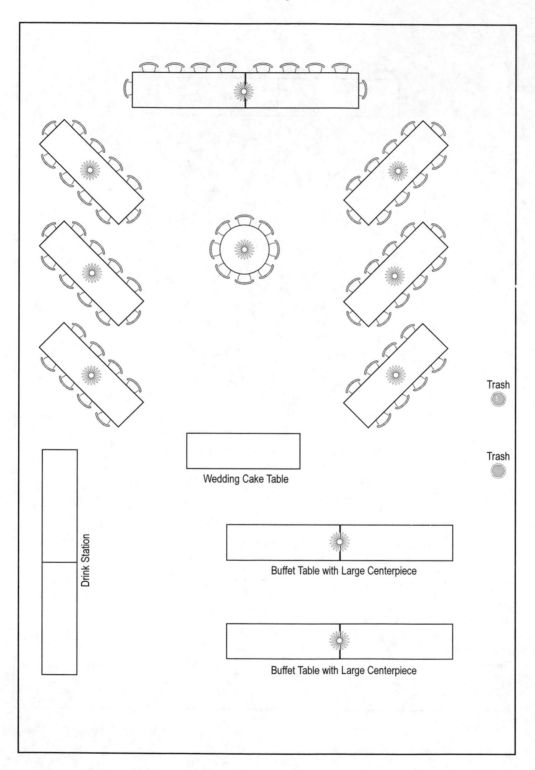

Brunch Buffet Table

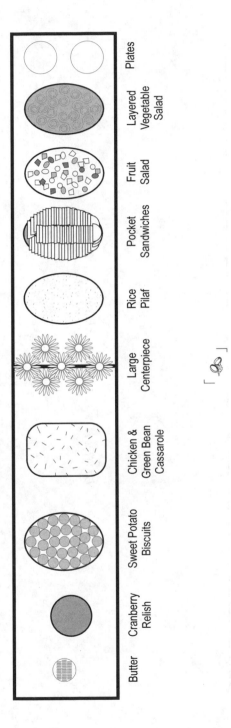

Butter · Cranberry Relish · Sweet Potato Biscuits · Chicken & Green Bean Casserole · Large Centerpiece · Rice Pilaf · Pocket Sandwiches · Fruit Salad · Layered Vegetable Salad · Plates

Brunch Wedding Cake Table

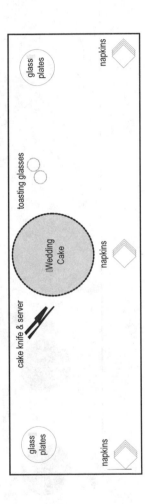

glass/plates · napkins · toasting glasses · Wedding Cake · cake knife & server · napkins · glass plates · napkins

Brunch Reception Drink Station

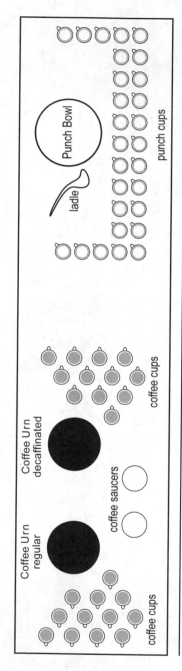

Coffee Urn regular

Coffee Urn decaffinated

coffee saucers

coffee cups

coffee cups

Punch Bowl

ladle

punch cups

Brunch Reception Place Setting

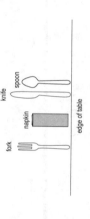

fork

napkin

knife

spoon

edge of table

 Chapter 7

The Dessert Reception

For the couple with a sweet tooth, it doesn't get any better than this! With everything from brownies to cheesecakes to candies, your guests will have nothing but sweet memories of your wedding day!

Because this plan features only desserts, it's best for middle-of-the-day receptions after your guests have eaten a meal or two. This probably isn't a wise choice for a reception that will take place during a traditional meal time because so much sugar on a hungry stomach may cause more than one case of indigestion.

Although this is one of the easier reception plans in this book, it can require the greatest number of helpers—15 to 29. It's not because there's so much work to be done; it's simply a matter of logistics. Only so many baking pans can fit into an oven at one time, and home refrigerators only have enough space for so many pie pans. If your helpers have access to a larger-than-normal amount of oven and/or fridge space, you can cut down on the number of helpers you'll need. Another option for reducing your helper needs: Ask some helpers to make more than one item. Everything on the menu can be made a day or two ahead of time. If your helpers are willing, they can make a couple of menu items over two or three days.

The Menu

Peanut Butter Chocolate Chip Cookies
Crème de Menthe Miniature Brownies
Cream Cheese Butter Mints
Old-Fashioned Taffy
Chocolate-Covered Cherries
Key Lime Pie
Chocolate Mousse
Southern Pecan Pie
Rum Cake
Carrot Cake
Miniature Cheesecakes
Freshly Brewed Regular and Decaffeinated Coffee
Citrus Fruit Punch

The Helpers

You'll need 14 teams—15 to 29 people—to help with this reception. With the exception of the setup/take-down, coffee, and punch teams, all jobs require only basic baking skills and one or two people per team. If some of your helpers are willing to double up and prepare two items, the best combinations are Peanut Butter Chocolate Chip Cookies and Cream Cheese Butter Mints; Creme de Menthe Miniature Brownies and Southern Pecan Pie; and Old-Fashioned Taffy and Chocolate-Covered Cherries. Ask the Butter Mints team to cut and serve the wedding cake.

Setup/Take-Down Team: You'll need two or three people to set up the tables and chairs and to lay out tablecloths and decorations. When the reception is over, they'll take everything down.

Coffee Team: If they can fill a pot with water and flip a switch, they can make the coffee. This team requires only one or two people.

Punch Team: Recruit one or two people for this job that's only marginally more difficult than making coffee.

With the exception of the setup/take-down team and the coffee and punch teams, all jobs require only basic baking skills and one or two people per team. If some of your helpers are willing to double up and prepare two items, the best combinations are Peanut Butter Chocolate Chip Cookies and Cream Cheese Butter Mints; Creme de Menthe Miniature Brownies and Southern Pecan Pie; and Old Fashioned Taffy and Chocolate Covered Cherries. Ask the Butter Mints team to cut and serve the wedding cake.

The Hardware

In addition to recruiting the people who will help you with your reception, you'll need to rent or purchase the items listed on page 148. Before whipping out your credit card, however, ask your reception site representative if he or she can provide any of the items free of charge or at a discount. You may also be able to borrow many of the items from friends and family members and save yourself some serious money. See Chapter 9 for complete information on renting or otherwise acquiring the supplies listed here.

Included in this list are white table linens, centerpieces, floral arrangements, and candelabras. These are staples at traditional wedding receptions, but you may want to use some other type of decorations. Chapter 8 is packed with decorating ideas you may want to consider.

Number of guests	50	100	150
60" round tables	7	7	13
8' x 30" banquet tables	8	8	8
36" round tables	1	1	1
White Samsonite chairs	50	100	150
120" round white tablecloth	7	7	13
90" round white tablecloths	1	1	1
54" x 120" white tablecloths	8	8	8
21' white skirting segments	6	6	6
5-gal. punch fountain	1	1	1
5-oz. glass punch cups	75	125	175
90-cup stainless steel coffee urns	2	2	2
Coffee cups	35	75	100
Coffee saucers	35	75	100
Sugar bowls	4	4	4
Creamers	2	2	2
Spoons	35	75	100
Forks	75	75	175
8" glass plates	75	75	175
Floral centerpiece for buffet	1	1	1
Floral centerpieces for guest tables	7	7	6
Floral centerpiece for coffee table	1	1	1
Floral arrangement for guest register table	1	1	1
Wedding cake	1	1	1
Cake knife and server	1 set	1 set	1 set
Engraved napkins	125	250	400
Guest book and pen	1 set	1 set	1 set
Toasting glasses	1 set	1 set	1 set

*Note: Have your rentals delivered the day **before** the reception. You don't want your setup team waiting around for a delivery. All items should be there when the team arrives so that they can immediately start setting up.*

Reception Team Job Descriptions

Team 1: Setup/Take-Down Team

Helper #1 _____

Helper #2 _____

Helper #3 _____

Reception Coordinator _____

Reception Location _____

Time of Ceremony _____

Number of Guests _____

Responsibilities

   Clean out two large plastic trash cans for use at the reception. Because these will be seen by guests, try to find cans that are presentable. Be sure to bring about a half dozen trash can liners.

   Arrive at the reception site about four hours before the ceremony to arrange tables and chairs in their designated locations (see the Dessert Reception room diagram on pages 172 to 174).

   Place tablecloths and skirting on tables as follows:

- **For 50 or 100 guests:** Four 8' x 30" tables (Wedding Cake, Gift, Coffee, and Punch Tables) and 54" x 120" tablecloths. Clip skirting on *before* laying the tablecloth on the table. Four 8' x 30" tables (buffet tables) and 54" x 120" tablecloths— place tablecloths on tables, push tables together, and attach skirting around the perimeter of the Dessert Table. Seven 60" round tables (120" round tablecloths) for dining tables— no skirting required. One 36" round table (90" round table- cloth) for guest register table—no skirting required.

- **For 150 guests:** Four 8' x 30" tables (wedding cake, gift, coffee, and punch tables) and 54" x 120" tablecloths. Clip skirting on *before* laying the tablecloth on the table. Four 8' x 30" tables (buffet tables) and 54" x 120" tablecloths—place tablecloths on tables, push tables together, and attach skirt- ing around the perimeter of the dessert table. Thirteen 60" round tables (120" round tablecloths) for dining tables—no skirting required. One 36" round table (90" round tablecloth) for guest registry table—no skirting required.

❧ If more than one color will be used on the tables, the bride will let you know how the linens should be arranged.

❧ The bride will provide items such as dishes, silverware, the punch fountain, and centerpieces and have them delivered to the reception site. Using the diagrams for the Buffet Table, Wedding Cake Table, Punch Table, Coffee Table, and Guest Register Table (see pages 175 to 177), arrange the items on the appropriate tables.

❧ During the reception, help keep the area neat and clean. Keep an eye on the trash cans and replace the liners when they get full.

❧ At the end of the reception, help with clean up and return rented items to the location of the room where they were delivered.

Team 2: Peanut Butter Chocolate Chip Cookies Team

Helper #1: _____

Helper #2: _____

Reception Coordinator _____

Reception Location _____

Time of Ceremony _____

Number of Guests _____

Responsibilities

❧ Make the cookies the day before the reception using the recipe on page 151.

❧ Arrive at the reception site about 15 to 30 minutes before the wedding and place the trays of cookies on the buffet tables as shown on the Buffet Table diagram on page 175.

❧ Keep an eye on the cookie trays during the reception and replenish them when necessary.

❧ At the end of the reception, help with clean up.

Shopping List

Number of guests	50	100	150
Butter or margarine, softened	¾ cup	1½ cups	2¼ cups
Shortening	¼ cup	½ cup	¾ cup
Sugar	¾ cup	1½ cups	2¼ cups
Brown sugar, packed firm	¾ cup	1½ cups	2¼ cups
Eggs	2	4	6
Vanilla extract	1 tsp.	2 tsp.	3 tsp.
All-purpose flour	2¼ cups	4½ cups	6¾ cups
Baking soda		1 tsp.	2 tsp.
3 tsp.			
Salt	¼ tsp.	½ tsp.	¾ tsp.
Peanut butter chips	1 cup	2 cups	3 cups
Semisweet chocolate chips (6 oz pack)	1	2	3
Yield	6 dozen	12 dozen	18 dozen
20" round serving trays	2	2	2
Small tongs	4	4	4

Peanut Butter Chocolate Chip Cookies

With an electric mixer, cream together the butter and shortening. Slowly add both sugars. Add eggs and vanilla; mix well.

In a separate bowl, combine flour, salt, and baking soda; mix well. Add flour mixture to butter mixture and continue mixing.

Remove mixing blades and stir in peanut butter and chocolate chips by hand.

Using a teaspoon, drop large spoonfuls of dough onto ungreased cookie sheets. Bake at 375 degrees for 9 to 11 minutes. Remove from oven and allow to cool.

When completely cool, arrange the cookies on your trays and cover with plastic wrap. If you have extra cookies that won't fit on the trays, place them on plates, cover them with plastic wrap, and use them to replenish the trays during the reception.

Team 3: Crème de Menthe Brownies Team

Helper #1 _____

Helper #2 _____

Reception Coordinator _____

Reception Location _____

Time of Ceremony _____

Number of Guests _____

Responsibilities

  ❧ Make the brownies the day before or early on the day of the reception using the recipes on page 153. Because the brownies need to be refrigerated, you might want to clean out your fridge ahead of time so you'll have plenty of room to store them.

  ❧ Arrive at the reception site about 15 to 30 minutes before the wedding and place the trays of brownies on the buffet tables as shown on the Buffet Table diagram on page 175. Your extra brownies should be refrigerated at the reception site. If no refrigerator is available, store them in a shady, cool spot out of direct sunlight.

  ❧ Keep an eye on the brownie trays during the reception and replenish them when necessary.

  ❧ At the end of the reception, help with clean up.

Shopping List

Number of guests	50	100	150
For Brownies			
Unsweetened chocolate (1 oz. squares)	1½	3	4½
Butter or margarine	1½ cups	3 cups	4½ cups
Eggs	6	12	18
Sugar	3 cups	6 cups	9 cups
All-purpose flour	1½ cups	3 cups	4½ cups
Salt	¾ tsp.	1½ tsp.	2¼ tsp.
Vanilla extract	1½ tsp.	3 tsp.	4½ t tsp.
Yield	6 dozen	12 dozen	18 dozen
Baking pans (13"x 9'x 2')	2	4	6

Number of guests	50	100	150
For Crème de Menthe Frosting			
Semisweet chocolate morsels	¾ cup	1½ cups	2¼ cups
Powdered sugar, sifted	6 cups	12 cups	18 cups
Butter or margarine, softened	¾ cup	1½ cups	2¼ cups
Half-and-half	3 oz.	6 oz.	9 oz.
Green Crème de Menthe	3 oz.	6 oz.	9 oz.
Walnuts, finely chopped	1½ cups	3 cups	4½ cups
20" round serving trays	2	2	2
Small tongs	4	4	4

Crème de Menthe Miniature Brownies

Combine the unsweetened chocolate and butter and cook over low heat until melted, stirring constantly. Remove from heat and let stand for 10 minutes.

With an electric mixer, beat the eggs until thick. Slowly add sugar while beating well. Add flour, salt, vanilla, and chocolate mixture. Beat for one minute.

Spoon the batter into lightly greased and floured baking pans. Bake at 350 degrees for 23 to 28 minutes or until a toothpick comes out clean. Cool for 10 minutes.

Spread Crème de Menthe frosting (recipethat follows) over entire area of the brownies and chill for four hours. Drizzle melted chocolate over frosting. Cut into small squares immediately.

Remove from pans and arrange brownies on your trays. (If you have extra brownies that won't fit on the trays, place them on plates and use them to replenish the trays during the reception.)

Let chill (uncovered) for 1½ hours. Wrap loosely with plastic wrap and return to the refrigerator.

Crème de Menthe Frosting

Combine all ingredients except for walnuts and beat on high speed until smooth.

Remove mixing blades and stir in nuts.

Team 5: Cream Cheese Butter Mints Team

Helper #1 _____

Helper #2 _____

Reception Coordinator _____

Reception Location _____

Time of Ceremony _____

Number of Guests _____

Responsibilities

- Make the butter mints the day before the reception using the recipe on pages 155. Because the butter mints need to be refrigerated, you might want to clean out your fridge ahead of time so you'll have plenty of room to store them.

- Arrive at the reception site about 15 to 30 minutes before the wedding, pour the mints into small bowls, and place them (and the serving spoons) on the buffet tables as shown on the Buffet Table diagram on page 175. The extra mints should be refrigerated at the reception site. If no refrigerator is available, store them in a shady, cool spot out of direct sunlight.

- Keep an eye on your mints during the reception. Make sure to replenish them when necessary.

- Help cut and serve the wedding cake.

- At the end of the reception, help with clean up.

Shopping List

Number of guests	50	100	150
Cream cheese, softened	3 oz.	6 oz.	9 oz.
Butter flavoring	2 tsp.	4 tsp.	6 tsp.
Peppermint extract	1/8 tsp.	¼ tsp.	3/8 tsp.
Powdered sugar, sifted	1 lb.	2 lbs.	3 lbs.
Yellow food coloring	Few drops	Few drops	Few drops
Yield	8 dozen	16 dozen	24 dozen
Glass candy bowls	2	2	2
Small serving spoons	2	2	2

Cream Cheese Butter Mints

With an electric mixer on low speed, beat cream cheese, butter flavoring, peppermint, and powdered sugar together.

Still mixing, slowly add yellow food coloring, drop by drop, until you get the color you like.

The mixture will be somewhat dry and crumbly—remove it from the mixing bowl and knead gently to soften it up.

Roll into small balls and slightly flatten with your finger. Place the finished mints into plastic baggies and refrigerate.

Team 5: Old-Fashioned Taffy Team

Helper #1 _____

Helper #2 _____

Reception Coordinator _____

Reception Location _____

Time of Ceremony _____

Number of Guests _____

Responsibilities

- Make the taffy the day before the reception using the recipe on pages 156. Because the taffy needs to be refrigerated, you might want to clean out your fridge ahead of time so you'll have plenty of room to store it.

- Arrive at the reception site about 15 to 30 minutes before the wedding, pour the taffy into small bowls, and place them (and the serving spoons) on the buffet tables as shown on the Buffet Table diagram on page 175. The extra taffy should be refrigerated at the reception site. If no refrigerator is available, store it in a shady, cool spot out of direct sunlight.

- Keep an eye on the taffy during the reception and replenish it when necessary.

- At the end of the reception, help with clean up.

Shopping List

Number of guests	50	100	150
Sugar	5 cups	10 cups	15 cups
Water	1 cup	2 cups	3 cups
Vinegar	½ cup	1 cup	1½ cups
Butter or margarine	2 Tbsp.	4 Tbsp.	6 Tbsp.
Salt	1/8 tsp.	¼ tsp.	3/8 tsp.
Vanilla extract	1 tsp.	2 tsp.	3 tsp.
Yield	6½ dozen	13 dozen	19½ dozen
Glass candy bowls	2	2	2
Small serving spoons	2	2	2
Candy thermometer	1	1	1

Old-Fashioned Taffy

Combine all ingredients except for vanilla in a Dutch oven and stir gently over low heat until sugar dissolves. Cover and cook on medium heat for two to three minutes. Remove lid and continue to cook over medium heat without stirring until mixture reaches 270 degrees (soft-crack stage).

Remove from heat and stir in the vanilla.

Pour mixture onto a buttered pan or slab of marble. Leave to cool until manageable.

Butter your hands, pick up the candy, and begin pulling. You will pull dozens of times until it becomes difficult to continue.

Divide candy in half. Pull and twist into the shape of a long rope approximately 1" in diameter. Cut into 1" pieces and arrange on a cookie sheet. Refrigerate for one hour.

Remove from refrigerator and place taffy in plastic baggies. Return to refrigerator.

Team 6: Chocolate-Covered Cherries Team

Helper #1 _____

Helper #2 _____

Reception Coordinator _____

Reception Location _____

Time of Ceremony _____

Number of Guests _____

Responsibilities

- Make the cherries the day before the reception using the recipe on page 158 (the cherries will stay fresh for one day only). Because the cherries need to be refrigerated, you might want to clean out your fridge ahead of time so you'll have plenty of room to store them.

- Arrive at the reception site about 15 to 30 minutes before the wedding and place the trays of cherries and tongs on the buffet tables as shown on the Buffet Table diagram on page 175. Your extra cherries should be refrigerated at the reception site. If no refrigerator is available, store them in a shady, cool spot out of direct sunlight.

- Keep an eye on your trays during the reception and replenish them when necessary.

- At the end of the reception, help with clean up.

Shopping List

Number of guests	50	100	150
Butter (softened)	4 Tbsp.	8 Tbsp.	12 Tbsp.
Powdered sugar (sifted)	5 cups	10 cups	15 cups
Milk	1 Tbsp.	2 Tbsp.	3 Tbsp.
Vanilla extract	½ tsp.	1 tsp.	1 ½ tsp.
Maraschino cherries with stems	84	168	252
Semisweet chocolate chips (12 oz bag)	2	4	6
Shortening	2 Tbsp.	4 Tbsp.	6 Tbsp.
Yield	7 dozen	14 dozen	21 dozen
20" Round Trays	2	2	2
Tongs	4	4	4

Chocolate-Covered Cherries

Cream butter and sugar together. Blend in milk and vanilla. Chill for 2½ hours.

Drain the cherries and dry them off with paper towels.

Put the bowl with the butter-and-sugar mixture into a larger bowl of ice to keep it cool as you work. Press a small amount of the mixture around each cherry. Place the cherries on wax paper-lined cookie sheets. Refrigerate for two hours.

Mix together the chocolate chips and shortening in a double boiler. Cook until chocolate has melted.

Holding the stems, dip the cherries one by one into the chocolate. Place on wax paper-lined cookie sheets. Return chocolate covered cherries to refrigerator until hard.

Remove the cherries from the cookie sheets and arrange them on your trays. If you have extra cherries, place them on a cookie sheet and use them to replenish the trays during the reception. Keep refrigerated until you are ready to leave.

Team 7: Key Lime Pie Team

Helper #1 _____

Helper #2 _____

Reception Coordinator _____

Reception Location _____

Time of Ceremony _____

Number of Guests _____

Responsibilities

- Make the pies the day before the reception using the recipe on page 159. Because the pies need to be refrigerated, you might want to clean out your fridge ahead of time so you'll have plenty of room to store them.

❧ Arrive at the reception site about 15 to 30 minutes before the wedding and place the pies and pie spatulas on the buffet tables as shown on the Buffet Table diagram on page 175. The extra pies should be refrigerated at the reception site. If no refrigerator is available, store them in a shady, cool spot out of direct sunlight.

❧ Keep an eye on the pies during the reception and replenish them after the first group of pies is depleted.

❧ At the end of the reception, help with clean up.

Shopping List

Number of pies	4	8	12
8" pie plates	4	8	12
Graham cracker crumbs	1 qt.	2 qts.	3 qts.
Butter, melted	½ cup	1 cup	1½ cups
Egg yolks	20	40	60
Condensed milk	8 cans	16 cans	24 cans
Lime juice	1 qt.	2 qts.	3 qts.
Grated lime rind	1 lime	2 limes	3 limes
Yield	24 slices	48 slices	72 slices
Pie spatulas	4	4	4

Key Lime Pie

Note: The following recipe makes one Key Lime Pie—your mixer may not be big enough to handle the filling for all the pies at one time. For 50 guests, make four pies. For 100 guests, make eight pies. For 150 guests, make 12 pies.

Recipe for one Key Lime Pie:

1 cup graham cracker crumbs 2 tbsp. butter, melted
5 egg yolks 2 cans condensed milk
1 cup lime juice Rind of ¼ lime, grated
1-8" pie plate

Mix together the graham cracker crumbs and butter. Press the mixture into 8' pie plates. Bake for two minutes at 350 degrees. Remove from oven. Beat the egg yolks until light and fluffy. Add condensed milk to yolks. Fold in the lime juice and rind. Pour mixture into pie shells. Refrigerate two hours or until chilled and firm. Cover with plastic wrap and refrigerate.

Team 8: Chocolate Mousse Team

Helper #1 _____

Helper #2 _____

Reception Coordinator _____

Reception Location _____

Time of Ceremony _____

Number of Guests _____

Responsibilities

❧ Make the mousse the day before the reception using the recipe on page 161. Because the mousse needs to be refrigerated, you might want to clean out your fridge ahead of time so you'll have plenty of room to store it.

❧ Arrive at the reception site about 15 to 30 minutes before the wedding and place the bowls of mousse on the buffet tables as shown on the Buffet Table diagram on page 175. The extra mousse should be refrigerated at the reception site. If no refrigerator is available, store it in a shady, cool spot out of direct sunlight.

❧ Keep an eye on the bowls of mousse during the reception and replenish them when they're empty.

❧ At the end of the reception, help with clean up.

Shopping List

Gallons of mousse	2	4	6
Sugar	4 cups	8 cups	12 cups
Water	2 cups	4 cups	6 cups
Egg yolks	30	60	90
Strong coffee	2½ cups	5 cups	7½ cups
Grand Marnier (orange liqueur)	½ cup	1 cup	1½ cups
Butter (room temperature)	1 lb.	2 lbs.	3 lbs.
Semisweet chocolate chips, 12 oz bag	5	10	15
Egg whites	16	32	48
Heavy cream	2 qts.	4 qts.	6 qts.
5-6 qt. glass bowls	2	4	6
Large serving spoons	4	4	4
Yield	60 servings	120 servings	180 servings

Chocolate Mousse

In a large pot, bring sugar and water to a boil. Cook for 4½ minutes.

In a double boiler, whip egg yolks until light and fluffy. While whipping, slowly add sugar-and-water mixture to the egg mixture. Add coffee and liqueur and continue to whip. Add butter.

Melt chocolate in a double boiler and stir it into the mixture.

Beat the egg whites until stiff and fold them into the mixture.

Beat heavy cream until stiff and fold into the mixture. Pour mousse into your serving bowls, cover with plastic wrap, and refrigerate.

Team 8: Southern Pecan Pie Team

Helper #1 _____

Helper #2 _____

Reception Coordinator _____

Reception Location _____

Time of Ceremony _____

Number of Guests _____

Responsibilities

❧ Make the pies the day before the reception using the recipe on page 162. Because the pies need to be refrigerated, you might want to clean out your fridge ahead of time so you'll have plenty of room to store them.

❧ Arrive at the reception site about 15 to 30 minutes before the wedding and place the pies on the buffet tables as shown on the Buffet Table diagram on page 175. Your extra pies should be refrigerated at the reception site. If no refrigerator is available, store them in a shady, cool spot out of direct sunlight.

❧ Keep an eye on the pies during the reception and replenish them after the first group of pies is depleted.

❧ At the end of the reception, help with clean up.

Shopping List

Number of pies	4	8	12
Unbaked 9' pie shell	4	8	12
Eggs	12	24	36
Dark corn syrup	4 cups	8 cups	12 cups
Sugar	2 cups	4 cups	6 cups
Butter (melted)	8 oz.	1 lb.	1½ lbs.
Vanilla extract	2 Tbsp.	4 Tbsp.	6 Tbsp.
Pecan halves (chopped coarsely)	1 lb.	2 lbs.	3 lbs.
Yield	32 slices	64 slices	96 slices
Pie spatulas	2	2	2

Southern Pecan Pie

Note: The following recipe makes one Southern Pecan Pie—you may not have enough oven space to bake all the pies you'll need at one time. For 50 guests, make four pies. For 100 guests, make eight pies. For 150 guests, make 12 pies.

Recipe for one Southern Pecan Pie

1 unbaked pie shell	3 eggs
1 cup dark corn syrup	1/2 cup sugar
1/4 cup butter, melted	1 1/2 tsp. vanilla
1/2 cup pecan halves, chopped	

Bake pie shells at 450 degrees for five to seven minutes. Remove from oven. Beat eggs well. Add corn syrup, sugar, butter, and vanilla to the beaten eggs. Pour mixture into the pie shells. Sprinkle pecans over the top of the pies. Bake at 325 degrees for 45 minutes. Allow pies to cool at room temperature for 1½ hours. Cover with plastic wrap and refrigerate.

Team 8: Rum Cake Team

Helper #1 _____

Helper #2 _____

Reception Coordinator _____

Reception Location _____

Time of Ceremony _____

Number of Guests _____

Responsibilities

  ❦ Make the cakes the day before the reception using the recipes on pages 163 and 164. Because the cakes need to be refrigerated, you might want to clean out your fridge ahead of time so you'll have plenty of room to store them.

  ❦ Arrive at the reception site about 15 to 30 minutes before the wedding and place the cakes on the buffet tables as shown on the Buffet Table diagram on page 175. The extra cakes should be refrigerated at the reception site. If no refrigerator is available, store them in a shady, cool spot out of direct sunlight.

  ❦ Keep an eye on the cakes during the reception. Make sure to replenish them when necessary.

  ❦ At the end of the reception, help with clean up.

Shopping List

Number of cakes	4	8	12
For Rum Cake			
Butter (not margarine, room temp.)	2 lbs.	4 lbs.	6 lbs.
Sugar	8 cups	16 cups	24 cups
Eggs	16	32	48
All-purpose flour (sifted)	7 lbs.	14 lbs.	21 lbs.
Baking powder	4 Tbsp.	8 Tbsp.	12 Tbsp.
Salt	1 tsp.	2 tsp.	3 tsp.
Milk	1 qt.	2 qts.	3 qts.
Rum extract	1 Tbsp.	2 Tbsp.	3 Tbsp.
Baking tube pans	4	8	12
Cake plates	4	8	12
Cake knives	2	2	2

Number of cakes	4	8	12
For Rum Glaze			
Brown sugar, firmly packed	2 lbs.	4 lbs.	6 lbs.
Granulated sugar	2 lbs.	4 lbs.	6 lbs.
Butter	½ cup	1 cup	1½ cups
Water	4 cups	8 cups	12 cups
Salt	1/8 tsp.	¼ tsp.	3/8 tsp.
Rum	½ cup	1 cup	1½ cups
Yield	48 slices	96 slices	144 slices

Rum Cake

Note: The following recipe makes one Rum Cake—you may not have enough oven space to bake all the cakes you'll need at one time. For 50 guests, make four cakes. For 100 guests, make eight cakes. For 150 guests, make 12 cakes.

Recipe for one Rum Cake

1 lightly floured tube cake pan

1 cup butter	2 cups sugar
4 eggs	3½ cups all-purpose flour, sifted
3 tsp. baking powder	1/4 tsp. salt
1 cup milk	1 tsp. rum extract

Rum Cake Glaze for 1 cake

1 cup brown sugar, firmly packed	1 cup granulated sugar
2 Tbsp. butter	1 cup water
1 pinch salt	2 Tbsp. rum

In a large mixing bowl, beat butter and sugar together. Slowly add eggs while beating continually. In a separate bowl, combine the flour, baking powder, and salt and sift three times. Add alternately with milk to the butter-and-sugar mixture. Keep sides of bowl scraped well to insure a thorough mix. Add rum extract. Pour mixture into well-greased and floured tube pans. Bake at 325 degrees for 80 to 90 minutes or until wooden toothpick or wire comes out clean.

Rum Glaze:

Combine all ingredients except rum in a saucepan. Boil for four minutes then remove from heat. Add rum and mix well. Slowly pour half of the glaze over the cakes while they're still hot and in the pans. Let cakes cool. Flip cakes over onto cake plates and pour remaining glaze over them. Allow to finish cooling for one hour. Loosely cover cakes with plastic wrap and refrigerate.

Team 9: Carrot Cake Team

Helper #1 _____

Helper #2 _____

Reception Coordinator _____

Reception Location _____

Time of Ceremony _____

Number of Guests _____

Responsibilities

- ✎ Make the cakes the day before the reception using the recipe on pages 167. Because the cakes need to be refrigerated, you might want to clean out your fridge ahead of time so you'll have plenty of room to store them.

- ✎ Arrive at the reception site about 15 to 30 minutes before the wedding and place the cakes on the buffet tables as shown on the Buffet Table diagram on page 175. The extra cakes should be refrigerated at the reception site. If no refrigerator is available, store them in a shady, cool spot out of direct sunlight.

- ✎ Keep an eye on the cakes during the reception. Make sure to replenish them when necessary.

- ✎ At the end of the reception, help with clean up.

Shopping List

Number of cakes	4	8	12
Carrot Cake			
Grated carrots	12 cups	24 cups	36 cups
All purpose flour	8 cups	16 cups	24 cups
Baking powder	4 tsp.	8 tsp.	4 Tbsp.
Baking soda	8 tsp.	5¼ Tbsp.	8 Tbsp.
Salt	2 tsp.	4 tsp.	2 Tbsp.
Sugar	8 cups	16 cups	24 cups
Ground cinnamon	4 tsp.	8 tsp.	4 Tbsp.
Eggs, well beaten	16	32	48
Vegetable oil	5 cups	10 cups	15 cups
Vanilla extract	4 tsp.	8 tsp.	4 Tbsp.
Cake plates	4	8	12
Cake knives	2	2	2

Number of cakes	4	8	12
Cream Cheese Frosting			
Cream cheese (8 oz. package)	4	8	12
Butter or margarine (softened)	2 cups	4 cups	6 cups
Sifted powdered sugar	4 lbs.	8 lbs.	12 lbs.
Vanilla extract	4 tsp.	8 tsp.	4 Tbsp.
Yield	48 slices	96 slices	144 slices

Carrot Cake

Note: The following recipe makes one Carrot Cake—you may not have enough oven space to bake all the cakes you'll need at one time. For 50 guests, make four cakes. For 100 guests, make eight cakes. For 150 guests, make 12 cakes.

Recipe of one Carrot Cake

3 cups carrots, grated   2 cups all-purpose flour
1 tsp. baking powder   2 tsp. baking soda
1/2 tsp. salt   2 cups sugar
1 tsp.Ground cinnamon   4 eggs, well beaten
1 1/4 cups vegetable oil   1 tsp. vanilla
3 greased and floured 9" cake pans

Cream Cheese Icing for 1 Carrot Cake

1 8-oz.pkg. cream cheese, softened   1/2 cup butter or margarine,
1 16-oz. box powdered sugar, sifted   softened
1 tsp. vanilla

Combine the first seven ingredients. Stir in eggs, oil, and vanilla. Pour batter into three well-greased and floured 9-inch round cake pans. Bake at 350 degrees for 30 minutes or until a wooden toothpick or wire comes out clean. Cool in pans for 15 minutes. Remove from pans and let cool completely. Spread cream cheese frosting (see recipe on this page) between the layers and on top of the cakes. Refrigerate frosted cakes uncovered until ready to leave for reception. (Cover with plastic wrap while transporting.)

Cream Cheese Frosting

Combine the cream cheese and butter and whip till smooth. Add powdered sugar and vanilla. Beat until light and fluffy.

Team 9: Miniature Cheesecakes Team

Helper #1 _____

Helper #2 _____

Reception Coordinator _____

Reception Location _____

Time of Ceremony _____

Number of Guests _____

Responsibilities

✑ Make the cheesecakes the day before the reception using the recipes on page 168. Because the cheesecakes need to be re-frigerated, you might want to clean out your fridge ahead of time so you'll have plenty of room to store them.

✑ Arrive at the reception site about 15 to 30 minutes before the wedding and place the cheesecakes on the buffet tables as shown on the Buffet Table diagram on page 175. The extra cheesecakes should be refrigerated at the reception site. If no refrigerator is available, store them in a shady, cool spot out of direct sunlight.

✑ Keep an eye on the cheesecakes during the reception. Make sure to replenish them when necessary.

✑ At the end of the reception, help with clean up.

Shopping List

Number of guests	50	100	150
Graham cracker crumbs	1½ cups	3 cups	4½ cups
Butter or margarine (melted)	6 Tbsp.	¾ cup	1 cup + 2 Tbsp.
Cream cheese (8 oz. pkg., softened)	3	6	9
Sugar	¾ cup	1½ cups	2¼ cups
Eggs	3	6	9
Vanilla extract	1½ tsp.	3 tsp.	4½ tsp.
Strawberry preserves	6 Tbsp.	¾ cup	1 cup + 2 Tbsp.
20" serving trays	2	2	2
1 dozen muffin pans	6	12	18
Miniature paper liners	72	144	216
Yield	6 dozen	12 dozen	18 dozen

Miniature Cheesecakes

Combine the graham cracker crumbs and butter and stir well.

Line 1¾' muffin pans with miniature paper liners. Spoon 1 teaspoon of graham cracker mix into each paper liner and gently mash down.

Using an electric mixture, beat cream cheese on high speed until light and fluffy. Slowly add sugar. Add egg and vanilla and beat well.

Spoon mixture on top of graham cracker crumbs in the paper liners. Bake at 350 degrees for 10 minutes.

Spoon ¼ teaspoon of strawberry preserves on top of each cheesecake. Arrange the cheesecakes on your trays. Place any extras on cookie sheets; you'll use these to replenish the trays during the reception. Cover with plastic wrap and refrigerate.

Team 9: Coffee Team

Helper #1 _____

Helper #2 _____

Reception Coordinator _____

Reception Location _____

Time of Ceremony _____

Number of Guests _____

Responsibilities

- Make small placards or signs for regular and decaffeinated coffee. You may want to make these on your computer or write them using calligraphy.

- The coffee will take 30 minutes to an hour to brew. Arrive at the reception site in plenty of time for the coffee to be ready by the beginning of the reception. The coffee urns will be waiting for you at the reception site.

❧ Using the Coffee Table diagram on page 178, place the small bowls and creamers in their assigned spots. Fill half the bowls with sugar and the other half with sweetener packets. Fill the creamers with half-and-half. Place the coffee signs/placards in front of the appropriate coffee urn. Place back-up supplies under the table.

❧ During the reception, keep an eye on the coffee table and replenish sugar, cream, and so forth when necessary.

❧ At the end of the reception, help with clean up.

Shopping List

Number of guests	50	100	150
Regular coffee (16 oz. can)	½	¾	1
Decaffeinated coffee (16 oz. can)	½	¾	1
Water per pot	50 cups	75 cups	90 cups
Sugar	1 lb.	1½ lbs.	2 lbs.
Sweet 'N Low (packets)	50	75	100
Equal (packets)	25	35	50
Cream (half-and-half)	2 qts.	3 qts.	4 qts.
Glass bowls (softball size)	6	6	6
Regular sign	1	1	1
Decaffeinated sign	1	1	1
12' three-pronged extension cords	2	2	2

Coffee

At the reception site, make sure that the coffee table is located near electrical outlets. You may have to move the table closer to an outlet if you don't have easy access. Use your extension cords if necessary.

Remove the lids, filters, and stems from the coffee pots. Fill the pots to the correct water line (look for lines inside the pots). Reinsert the stems and filters. Fill the filters with the desired amount of coffee (read the labels on the coffee can to find out how much coffee to measure into the filters). Secure the lids and turn the coffee urns on. The coffee will take from 30 minutes to an hour to brew.

Team 10: Punch Team

Helper #1 _____

Helper #2 _____

Reception Coordinator _____

Reception Location _____

Time of Ceremony _____

Number of Guests _____

Responsibilities

- Gather all ingredients for the punch and arrive at the reception site one hour before the wedding. Decide ahead of time where you're going to get the ice and pick it up on your way to the reception site. Make the punch at the reception site according to the recipe on page 171.

- Fill the punch fountain with punch and keep it replenished during the reception. The fountain will be waiting for you at the hall, but you'll need to bring an extension cord (see Shopping List) in case the fountain's cord won't easily reach an outlet.

- At the end of the reception, help with clean up.

Shopping List

Number of guests	50	100	150
Cranberry juice (64 oz. bottle)	3	5	7
Pineapple juice (46 oz. can)	4	6	8
Orange juice (2 qt. carton)	2	4	6
Ginger ale (2 liter bottle)	4	7	9
Almond extract	4 Tbsp.	6 Tbsp.	8 Tbsp.
Orange slices	3 oranges	5 oranges	7 oranges
Bagged ice (10 lb. bags)	5	7	10
Large ice chest	2	2	3
Clean 5-gallon buckets	2	2	3
Clean 1-gallon buckets	2	2	2
Large spoon (to mix punch)	1	1	1

Citrus Punch

In the 5-gallon buckets, combine cranberry juice, pineapple juice, orange juice, and almond extract (divided equally among the buckets).

Just before the reception, add ginger ale to the mix.

Because the 5-gallon buckets will be too heavy and cumbersome to lift easily, fill the 1-gallon buckets with punch and pour into the punch fountain. (The fountain will be waiting for you at the reception site.) Use the smaller buckets to refill the fountain during the reception. Store buckets of punch under the table.

Slice oranges ¼" thick and float them on top of the punch.

Always add ice directly to the punch fountain, not to the 1- or 5-gallon buckets. Store ice (in an ice chest) under the table.

Dessert Reception for 50 Guests

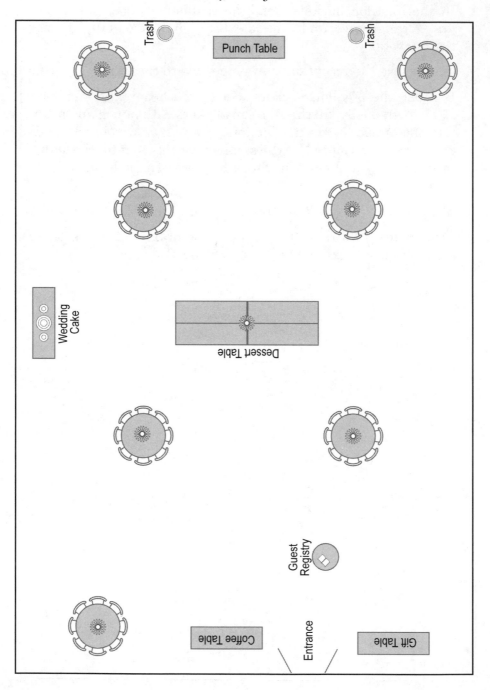

Dessert Reception for 100 Guests

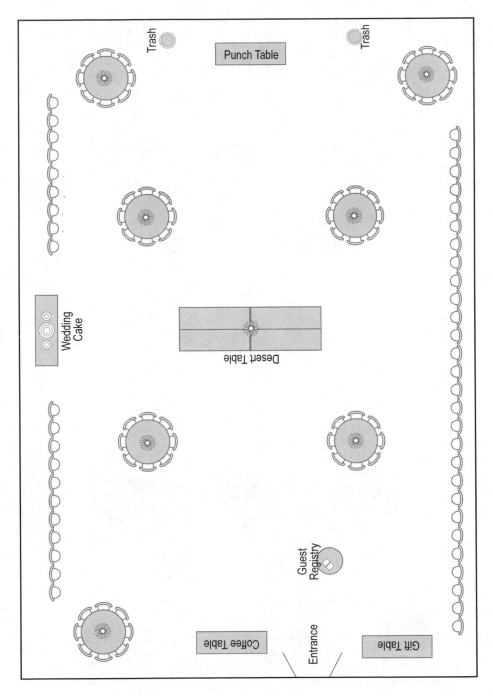

Dessert Reception for 150 Guests

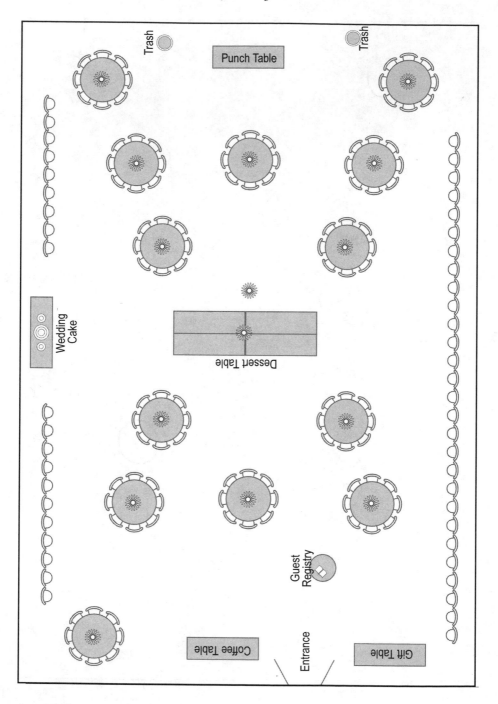

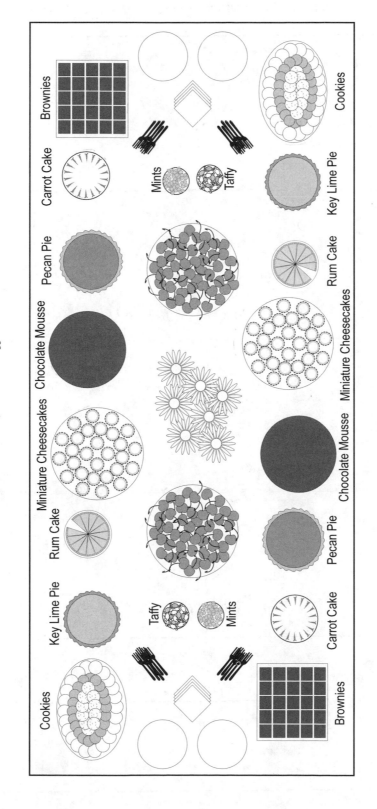

Dessert Reception Buffet Table

Dessert Reception Wedding Cake Table

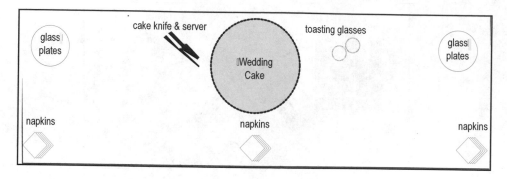

Dessert Reception Coffee Service Table

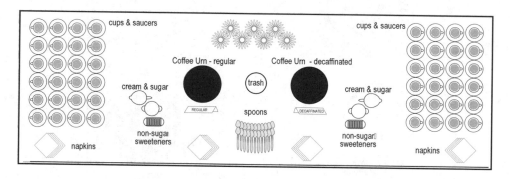

Dessert Reception Punch Table

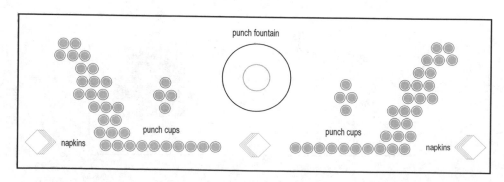

Dessert Reception Guest Registry Table

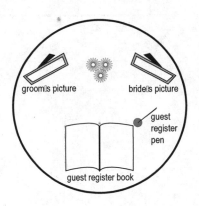

 *Chapter 8*

Special Touches

There's a drive-in restaurant in Boise, Idaho, that is owned and operated by a chef. Every Friday and Saturday night, it serves prime rib dinners with all the trimmings—baked potato, salad, warm roll. You'd be hard-pressed to find a better prime rib dinner anywhere in the state of Idaho, and every weekend cars line up five and six deep at the drive-through windows. To be honest, though, the splendor fizzles a bit when you get home and pull the Styrofoam to-go box out of the paper bag and dig in with a set of plastic utensils. It still tastes good, but it would taste even better if a sexy, blonde waiter named Chad sauntered to your table, set it in front of you on a china plate, and flashed you a million-dollar smile.

So what does the prime rib dinner from a drive-in restaurant in Boise have to do with your wedding reception? Just like the prime rib loses a hefty chunk of its pizzazz by the way it's served, the food you offer guests at your reception could come down a notch if you don't pay attention to the atmosphere you create around it. Presentation—Chad, if you will—makes all the difference in the world.

Now, no one's suggesting that you have to go out and buy gold-rimmed china and sterling flatware or your guests will tell their friends you gave a poor reception. Beautiful presentation doesn't mean you have to kiss the budget goodbye. Special touches and attention to detail can add more to the overall impression your reception makes than all the sparkling crystal in the world. All it takes is creativity.

How much creativity depends on the facility you've chosen and the vision you have for your reception. Many venues are already beautifully appointed and don't need much more than a vase of fresh flowers and a few strings of twinkle lights to make them work. On the other end of the spectrum, the best thing you can say about some places is that they have walls and a roof. If your reception site falls into this category, don't assume your only hope is to get your guests liquored up so they won't notice how dull the place is. Remember that story about the ugly duckling who turned into a graceful swan? You can make the same kind of transformation happen with your reception venue, regardless of what it looks like now. Even the most aesthetically challenged hall or room can become a place of magic and beauty on your special day.

In the reception plan chapters (Chapters 2 through 7), you'll find recommendations for elegant, traditional decorations and table arrangements—tablecloths and skirts, candelabras, and flowers. This type of setup will always be beautiful and may be exactly what you want, so you might not even consider doing anything else. But if traditional is the last word you'd use to describe your style, or if you're looking for some unique decorating ideas, this chapter will be one of your favorites.

Before you order a single iris or buy your first votive, do a little prep work. Visit your reception venue at the time of day or evening that your reception will be held and take a good look around. What is the lighting like? Will you need to cover any windows to block a glaring sun? Do the light fixtures have dimmer switches or are your only lighting choices on or off? Will any features—an ugly wall or a bad ceiling, for example—fade into the background when the sun goes down and the lights are low? By checking out the reception-time lighting, you may find problem spots you didn't notice when you booked the place, or you may realize that you won't have to waste time and money camouflaging something that won't be noticed anyway.

While you're still at your reception spot, find out what the ground rules are. Can you use candles or have open flames? How much leeway do you have in hanging things on the walls or from the ceiling? Do fire codes or the venue's policies prohibit plugging things like twinkle lights into outlets, and what's the limit if they're allowed?

Also ask about any decorating items they may have for your use. If they host many wedding receptions, they may make candelabras, lattice panels, trellises, linens, potted trees, or other decorative items available. The person you deal with at the facility may even be able to give you some decorating ideas based on what other couples have already done. Sketch out a simple floor plan (or ask the site representatibe if one is printed up already), noting the room's measurements and the locations of windows, doors, columns or other structural features, electrical outlets, and any other unmovable objects you'll have to work around.

Armed with your sketch and base of information about the facility, sit down and figure out the look and feel you want to create. Remember, your reception and the food you serve should complement your wedding ceremony's tone and degree of formality. Your guests will scratch their heads in confusion, for example, if they go from your late-afternoon, barefoot-in-the-park ceremony to a formal crystal-and-china reception where you serve a brunch menu.

Think about the elements you want to use to convey the tone you've decided on. As you look through magazines, visit wedding-planning chat rooms, and talk with friends who've already married, you'll find lots of great decorating ideas. They may be so creative and clever that you'll want to incorporate them all into your reception décor.

Bad plan.

Have you ever seen a woman who piles on makeup—foundation, powder, blush, bright green eye shadow, eyeliner, eyebrow pencil, 12 coats of blue mascara, lipstick, lip pencil, and that glitter stuff that makes her face look like a Christmas ornament? She'd be beautiful with a little eye shadow and a dab of blush, but covered in all that makeup, she just looks tacky.

An overdecorated reception hall will look like that overdecorated woman. Unless tacky is the look you're going for, live by the less-is-more rule and choose decorating elements that will complement each other and advance the overall effect you're trying to achieve. Your reception décor should demonstrate your taste and style, not just your ability to fill a room with stuff.

Once you've decided on the look and feel you want, it's time to plan the specifics.

Setting the serving tables

Set the stage for your reception by dressing the focal point of the room—the tables that will hold the sumptuous food you'll serve. Now, anyone can throw a tablecloth over a table and slap a fruit tray and a centerpiece on top. But it's those little details and special touches that turn ho-hum table arrangements into ones that sparkle.

As noted earlier, your reception facility may provide basic tablecloths and skirts or you can get them at your local rental store. Linens provided by reception facilities are usually white and may not be in the best condition; rental stores generally carry them in a variety of colors. If white is too stark or plain solid colors just don't do it for you, try dressing them up a bit.

Overlays are an easy fix and add spots of color without overwhelming everything else in the room. Starting with your basic white or solid tablecloth (floor length or with a matching skirt that reaches the floor), place a large square of contrasting or complementary fabric diagonally across the center of the table, letting the corners hang down on the front and back sides of the table.

You can purchase square tablecloths for the overlays, but your choices will be fairly limited and store-bought linens can eat into your budget if you have a lot of tables to decorate. If you can sew a hem (or know someone who can), take a trip to your local fabric store and let your creative juices take over. You'll find tons of fabrics in a huge variety of colors, weights, textures, patterns, and price ranges. How about sheer overlays that add a subtle hint of color? Organza comes in a rainbow of colors and several different finishes—metallic, pearlized, iridescent—and makes stunning table accents. Lacy overlays on top of solid cloths can give a room an old-fashioned flair, especially with vases of fresh-from-the-garden roses rounding out the table décor.

For a more dramatic overlay, consider using lamé. This shimmering, metallic fabric comes in gold and silver, but you can also find it in deep shades like purple, blue, and red. Instead of laying it out smoothly, try puddling or bunching it on the table and setting your trays, baskets, and centerpiece among the waves and ripples you create. If you're looking to really dazzle your guests, make your overlays from confetti dot. This glamorous fabric, which comes in many colors, is covered in tiny metallic rounds that look like thousands of glistening sequins. Unfortunately, such unbridled glamour has a price—confetti dot will be very expensive if you need more than a few yards.

Depending on the look you want for your reception, you can use just about any fabric you see for overlays—florals, plaids, calicos, even seasonal fabrics. Don't limit yourself to fabrics sold by the bolt—use your imagination to come up with unique, original overlays. Quilts laid across tables that won't have food on them (gift table, guest register table, and so forth) or hung on walls bring a charming country touch. Sheets of mylar, available at theatrical supply shops, add dazzle and shine, while shawls or scarves lend a touch of class to the décor.

As you pick out your overlays, keep your other decorating elements in mind. If you choose a multicolored or patterned print, any dishes or centerpieces that sit on top should be fairly subtle—silver trays or solid-colored candles tied with gilded ribbons, for example. Conversely, the centerpiece that stands on a solid-colored overlay can be more elaborate or ornate. Be careful not to make both the overlay and centerpiece riots of wild color—they'll compete for the spotlight and end up looking overdone.

Another option for dressing up plain linens on the serving tables is draped fabric. (A word of caution: Don't drape and use overlays on the same tables—it's way too much.) Tulle is the most common fabric used for draping, and with good reason—it comes in a wide variety of colors, it falls beautifully, and it is inexpensive. Tulle is available in a wide range of common wedding colors, but if you look hard enough, you can find it in bolder shades or accented with glittery shapes like stars and dots.

There are two ways to drape a table. The first is simple and requires a relatively small amount of fabric. The second offers more versatility, but takes a bit more work. Both look spectacular.

- **Method 1:** Place a floor-length tablecloth over the table. Add a second tablecloth or length of fabric that reaches about halfway to the floor all the way around. (See the section on overlays for fabric ideas.) On the long sides of the table, measure 10 to 12 inches in from each end and mark with straight pins (for a round table, measure the entire perimeter, divide into equal sections, and mark with straight pins). At each marked spot, gather up the top cloth (starting from the hem) and pin with small safety pins near the top edge of the table. Attach bows, ribbon rosettes, or small floral accents at the top of each swag.

- **Method 2:** Cover the table with a floor-length tablecloth. Measure one long side of the table and multiply that number by 1 ½ or two—this is the length of fabric you'll need for the drape on that side. Divide the fabric (don't cut it!) into four equal sections and mark each section with a twistie. Divide the table into four sections and mark each section with a straight pin in the tablecloth (for a round table, measure the entire perimeter, divide into equal sections, and mark with straight pins). Pull the fabric up at the center and safety pin it to the tablecloth. Pull up and pin the ends of the fabric to the ends of the table in the same manner. Pull up and pin the fabric at each quarter mark (between the center and each end) to create four even swags across the length of the table. Repeat this process for the other three sides of the table so you have swags all around (the short ends have only one swag each). Attach bows, ribbon rosettes, or floral accents at the top of each swag to hide the pins.

Fabric isn't the only material you can use to drape a table—remember, we're being creative here. Maybe strands of beaded garland or thick satin cording festooned with tassels will give you the look you want. Or use tulle for your draping material but loosely wrap ivy garlands or white twinkle lights around it (use Method 2 for this treatment). Consider draping with garlands made of seasonal flowers and greenery, or if your wedding falls near the holidays, evergreen garlands intertwined with white twinkle lights.

Even without the garland, strings of twinkle lights attached to the perimeter of the table or woven into greenery running down the center of the table can put some zing into your arrangement. Your best bet is to buy battery-operated lights for the tables, especially the buffet tables. If battery-operated lights aren't available, tape cords to the floor. You don't want your guests to trip over cords as they fill their plates.

Sometimes dressing up plain tablecloths doesn't require drastic measures or elaborate decorations at all. Add visual interest to your table arrangement by elevating some of the objects on it to different heights. For example, place candelabras or floral arrangements on decorative columns, or serve some of the food items on tiered trays. Create platforms of varying heights to set your food trays on: Using one tablecloth as a base, place another tablecloth—identical or in a contrasting color or pattern—on top and slip a few inverted baking pans, milk crates, or sturdy boxes of differing sizes under the table-cloth. Don't pull the top cloth taut over the risers. Instead, let it fall and drape naturally over them, like a flowing, puddled tablecloth in a still life painting. Lightly sprinkle glitter or shiny, metallic confetti across the peaks and valleys for a dazzling punch of color.

Gift, guest register, wedding cake, and other utility tables

Although your utility tables don't have to be dressed exactly like your main serving tables, they should all look like they belong in the same room. Because it will be covered with boxes and bags before too long, detailed decorating will be lost on your gift table. Likewise, elaborate draping or garlanding will overwhelm a small guest regis-ter table, so you're better off keeping both tables relatively simple.

On the other hand, the wedding cake—the crowning glory of most receptions—can handle some extra attention, so go ahead and pull out all of the stops with that table. If you overlay, glitter, or drape your buffet tables, you can do the same to the one that holds your cake. You won't need a centerpiece—that's the cake's job—but you can bring in color by asking your bridesmaids to place their bou-quets in predetermined spots around the cake during the reception.

Guest tables

You can dress your guest tables exactly like your serving tables if you want, but linens that match or complement those on the buffet tables will look just as nice. With simpler table dressings, your guests will appreciate not having to navigate around all the fru-fru stuff—tulle drapes, ribbon rosettes, twinkle lights—to sit down, and you'll appreciate saving the money that all those extras would have cost.

To give your entire room an elegant feel without draping and garlanding every table, use floor-length tablecloths. Cover the tables in identical linens, or if you're decorating with more than one color, alternate the color of tablecloths throughout the room. Another option: Cover all of the guest tables in white and incorporate color with overlays, napkins, and centerpieces.

Centerpieces

If you're the creative type, you're going to love coming up with the centerpieces for your reception. While floral arrangements will never go out of style, your options for unique, personalized, or artful centerpieces are limitless. But first, a few guidelines:

- Because the serving table is the focal point of the room, the centerpiece that adorns it should be an eye-popper. If you go with floral arrangements as your centerpieces, the one on the buffet table should be the biggest and most elaborate of all the arrangements in the room. You may decide on an ice sculpture or mold for the buffet table centerpiece; be sure to choose one with enough oomph that it won't get lost among the trays, baskets, and bowls that will surround it.

- The centerpiece for the gift table, if you use a centerpiece at all, should be fairly small so it won't take up valuable space when the gifts start piling up.

- Centerpieces for the other utility tables should be proportionate to the tables themselves. The guest register table is small, so its centerpiece should be compact as well. Likewise, the long, rectangular coffee service table needs a centerpiece with some width—a tall, skinny vase of flowers would look too scrawny for such a large table.

- Centerpieces on guest tables should be built low enough that people sitting down can see over them to talk with guests on the other side of the table. Also remember that the guest tables will have plates, silverware, glasses, place cards (if you use them), and various other items on them, so don't overcrowd the limited space with massive, sprawling centerpieces.

- Guest table centerpieces don't have to be identical on every table. For example, you can use candle arrangements on some tables and baskets of flowers on others. Just make sure there's a common thread running through them, such as matching ribbon or the same color palette.

- Use unscented candles on buffet and guest tables—heavily fragranced candles will take away from the taste and smell of the food.

☙ Check with your reception site representative about the policy on candles. Some don't allow open flames, so you may have to use hurricane chimneys or brass lanterns to cover the flame.

If you want to use floral centerpieces, your best bet is to consult a florist who's experienced in doing weddings. He or she can help you decide what you need and design your arrangements. Be aware, though, that flowers—especially if the kind you want aren't in season—can be very expensive. If you want to use flowers but can't afford to outfit every table with them, buy arrangements for key areas such as the buffet table or head table and use something that complements the arrangements on the other tables.

Flowers are nice, but they're by no means your only option. With a little creativity and imagination, you can come up with center-pieces that are as unique as you are. Here are some ideas to get you going:

☙ Topiaries are easy to make and can be decorated with just about any kind of silk flowers. To make a topiary, glue floral foam into the base of a terra-cotta pot (if you want to paint or decorate the pot, do it before you put the topiary together). Cover the foam with moss and push a painted or ribbon-wrapped dowel into the foam. Push a floral foam ball onto the top of the dowel and cover it with moss. Press silk flowers (cut them about 1½ to 2 inches from the bud) into the ball and tie a wide ribbon into a bow right under the ball, letting the tails curl downward. Place the topiary on top of a puddled piece of tulle or other fabric.

☙ Baskets are versatile, inexpensive, and readily available. For a winter wedding, fill them with evergreen boughs, pinecones, nuts, apples, and cinnamon sticks. In spring, lay bundles of tulips in flat, beribboned baskets. For a summer wedding, line baskets with wedding-color fabric and fill with seashells, old bottles (corked with a rolled-up message inside), sand dollars, and a few pieces of coral. Fill baskets with apples, Indian corn, colored leaves, or small gourds to accent a fall reception.

☙ Arrange an assortment of pillar candles (various heights) and votives on a round or square mirror. Swirl strings of shiny bead or pearl garland around the base of the candles to add a little sparkle.

☙ Round up a variety of childhood photos of you and your fiancé and display them in frames on each table. (Make copies—don't use the originals, just in case someone spills a drink or one of your younger guests catches a tablecloth on fire.) Run an ivy gar-land down the middle of the table and nestle the framed photos among the leaves. If you'd like, print little placards with short descriptions and place them beside the photos (Examples: Lisa, at 9 years old, experiments with her mom's curlers. Twelve-year-old Joey and his first girlfriend.) Your guests will want to check out the photos at other tables, which can be a terrific ice breaker for guests when they start telling I-knew-them-when stories.

✦ Decorate your tables with potted plants like mums, tulips, or daffodils. Buy terra-cotta pots a size larger than the plastic containers the flowers are planted in and paint them to complement your other decorations. Place the flowers into the decorated pots before setting them on the table.

✦ Make centerpieces to reflect your or your fiancé's personality or interests. Is he a fireman? Incorporate helmets, stuffed dalmatians, and toy fire trucks into the centerpieces. Maybe you're a rodeo queen—decorate with cowboy boots full of wildflowers or staggered-height pillar candles encircled by a lariat intertwined with ivy or calico ribbon.

✦ Fill the bottom of medium-size wedding-color gift bags (with handles) with sand or another substance that will give it some weight. (A note about gift bags: You can find solid-colored, shiny bags in any discount store, but try specialty stationery shops and import stores for unique bags made of textured papers embedded with leaves or other materials. These usually come with a selection of coordinating tissue paper and other fillers.) Pinch sheets of tissue paper (in another wedding color or in silver or gold) in the center and fill the bag so that the tissue paper peeks out over the top (just like you'd put the paper in the bag if it had a gift in it). Tie a bouquet of three to five balloons (again in wedding or metallic colors) to one of the handles and sprinkle metallic confetti over the bag and onto the table around it. Be sure the ribbons on the balloons are long enough that the balloons will float about a yard over the table and won't obstruct your seated guests' view of each other.

✦ Bundle three pillar candles of staggered heights and tie them together with a bow. For an elegant look, use luxurious velvet ribbon. For a more casual feel, tie them together with raffia. Place the candles on a silver tray or right on the table with greenery underneath. To add sparkle, roll Styrofoam balls (in a variety of smaller sizes) in very fine silver or gold glitter and nestle them among the greenery.

✦ Let fresh fruit be the main attraction in your centerpieces. Lay greenery down the length of a rectangular banquet table, weaving in wedding-color ribbon. Place a large pillar or three-wick candle about every two feet and arrange fresh fruit—apples, grapes, oranges, plums, whatever looks good with your wedding colors—on the greenery in between the candles. Sprinkle metallic confetti over the greenery and fruit, with some spilling onto the tablecloth.

  Fill a fish bowl or pedestal bowl about three-quarters full of water and place colored aquarium gravel or decorative marbles in the bottom. Treat the water to make it inhabitable, then add a goldfish or two. Because you don't want cloudy water or—gasp!—dead fish floating belly up during your reception, put them in at the last minute. If you use pedestal bowls, tie a bow around the stem. Place the bowl on a bed of greenery or a small mirror, or scatter decorative marbles on the table around the base of the bowl. Let your guests take a centerpiece—and a new pet—home with them.

  Place a pillar candle inside a hurricane chimney. Arrange greenery, flowers, or a flower ring around the base for a simple but elegant centerpiece.

  Fill the base of a simple glass vase with colored decorator marbles and water. Put fresh flowers in the vase and place the vase on a small mirror and ring with votive candles. Scatter decorator marbles or sparkly confetti around the base of the vase and the votives.

  Artfully presented food makes a great centerpiece that your guests can savor with more than just their eyes. Line a basket with wedding-color fabric and fill it with delectable goodies like homemade breads and rolls, muffins, or pastries. To complete the edible centerpiece, scatter Hershey Kisses, which come wrapped in different colors in different seasons, around the basket.

  Fill glass bowls—round, pedestal, or fish bowls—half full of water and float candles or flowers in them. Specialty shops, wedding supply stores, and some department stores carry candles designed specifically for floating and in a number of colors and shapes. If you like, lightly tint the water with food coloring in one of your wedding colors. Place the bowls on mirrors and scatter decorator marbles or glitter around.

  Crumple tissue paper, or for a more dramatic look, colored plastic wrap (the kind you wrap baskets in, not the kind you wrap leftover fish in) and place in a glass champagne flute. Inflate three small balloons (two in one color, the third in a contrasting color) to about the size of an eggplant and attach to 12-inch white balloon sticks (these are available at wedding- and party-supply stores). Arrange the balloons in the flutes with the tissue paper or plastic wrap and tie curling ribbon around the stem of the flutes. Sprinkle confetti on the table around the arrangements. (For a more elegant look, use lace rounds—about nine inches in diameter—instead of tissue paper inside the flutes. Another option that will add sparkle is the shredded metallic filler that's sold beside the gift bags in stationery and party-supply stores.)

&. Decorate small grapevine wreaths with ribbon, strands of pearls, and flowers. Place a glass bowl in the center of the wreath. Half fill the bowl with decorator marbles and push a votive into the marbles so it won't tip over. Or fill the bowl halfway with water and float a flower or candle in it.

Room decorations

If table dressings and centerpieces are enough ornamentation for your reception site, your decorating is done. On the other hand, your site may be in need of some major cosmetic surgery. Help is on the way!

There are an infinite number of ways to dress up a boring, uninspiring, or even downright ugly room. If your reception will be held in the evening, the easiest and cheapest way is to turn out the lights! There's something mysterious and magical about candles and low lighting that appeals to just about everyone. Of course, you don't want the lights to be so low that your guests have to carry a flashlight to find the restroom.

If you want your reception hall to do a vanishing act, make candles a major element in your guest table centerpieces—maybe groupings of five to seven staggered-height pillar candles on silver or gold trays. Use candelabras (elevated on columns so guests won't burn themselves or catch their sleeves on fire as they reach for food) on the buffet tables. Incorporate white twinkle lights wherever you can—stretched loosely across the ceiling, around the perimeter of the serving tables, wrapped around columns, and intertwined with garlands hanging on the walls or above doors. You might even experiment with icicle lights—perhaps they'd look terrific attached to the ceiling over the dance floor. Plan ahead so you can catch some great deals on twinkle lights during after-Christmas sales.

Candles and twinkle lights will provide a good amount of light, but you probably don't want to turn the overhead lights completely off. If your facility has dimmer switches, you (or someone on your reception team) can adjust the lighting right before people start arriving but after all of the candles, twinkle lights, tiki torches, or whatever you use are lit up. But what if your site doesn't come equipped with dimmers? Simply remove or loosen some of the bulbs until the lighting looks right. This will have to be done during setup; you don't want anyone climbing all over your perfectly set tables loosening bulbs as your guests arrive.

Romantic, low lighting isn't the only way you can turn a plain room into a wonder to behold. Here are some other ideas to get your creative juices flowing:

- Rent potted plants and trees from a nursery to set around the room. Nurseries charge a reasonable rate—much less than it would cost to buy floral arrangements—and most will deliver them to your reception site and pick them up afterward. Cover the pots in wedding-color foil or decorate pots a size larger than the ones the plants come in and plop them in when they're delivered. Wrap the branches of potted trees with twinkle lights and set them at the corners of the dance floor or anywhere you need an extra touch of light. Place potted plants on steps going into the reception hall and any place around the room that could use a little extra color.

- Balloons offer color, versatility, and affordability and can be used in a huge variety of ways to decorate your reception hall. Florists, wedding- or party-supply stores, and balloon artists can make elaborate creations such as arches, walls, and wall hangings. For do-it-yourself decorating, buy hundreds of wedding-color balloons and spools of matching ribbon, then rent a helium tank the day of the wedding. Fill the balloons, tie them with slightly curled ribbon, and set them loose to bounce and bump across the ceiling. They'll add color and fun, and they're a great way to hide a water-stained or ugly ceiling. Another balloon-decorating idea: Put together bouquets with five to seven balloons tied with different lengths of curling ribbon. Superglue a hook onto the bottom (inside) of a tall, thin galvanized flower bucket and tie the balloons' ribbons to the hook. Fill the buckets a few inches deep with rocks or sand to weigh it down, then add a layer of moss to cover the rocks/sand. Tie a wide-ribbon bow around the bucket. Set the bouquets at the corners of the dance floor or anywhere else you need some color.

- Make a canopy of tulle over the dance floor or the head table. Starting from the center of the ceiling, drape tulle out toward the corners of the hall. For an even more spectacular look, string white twinkle lights along the drape of the canopy.

- Tulle is a great—and inexpensive—decorating tool. Drape it around windows or wrap it around columns in the hall. Spice it up a bit by entwining twinkle lights or ivy garland with the tulle.

✌ Take a trip to the woods and cut dead, bare-branched trees (we're not talking redwoods, here—cut trees in sizes that your reception site can accommodate). Spray paint the trees white, gold, or silver, then sprinkle white, gold, or silver glitter over them. After everything is dry, wrap the branches in white twinkle lights (see page 192 for instructions on camouflaging the wires) and secure the lights with clear fishing line. Plant the trees in large pots (you can paint or decorate these as well) about half full of plaster of Paris to keep them steady and weigh them down. Place the sparkling trees around the room for a dazzling look.

✌ Decorate circular or heart-shaped grapevine wreaths with ribbon and/or silk flowers and hang them on bare walls around the room.

✌ For an evening wedding, line the walkway or steps into the reception hall with luminaries. To make a luminary, fill the bottom (to a depth of about two inches) of a small paper bag with sand and push a votive candle or tea light into the sand until it's steady and won't fall over. Make enough luminaries to place them about a foot apart on either side of the walkway and one on each side of each step. For luminaries that are fancier, wedding- or party-supply stores carry white bags with wedding-theme cutouts, such as hearts and doves.

✌ Autumn weddings are great to decorate for because you have so many natural elements to work with. Bundle corn stalks together with fall- or wedding-color ribbons and tie to columns or stand against walls. Stack hay bales so that you have a couple of "shelves" to arrange items such as pumpkins, gourds, nuts, and baskets of apples on. Scatter autumn leaves and berries on the hay bales and let some of the leaves spill onto the floor. Hollow out a few pumpkins and place mums of different colors inside; set these on the steps leading up to the reception site or use them to fill in any bare spots in the room.

✌ For a Christmastime wedding, group evergreen trees of different sizes together to create a miniforest (this is a great way to cover a bad wall). Wrap the trees with strings of white twinkle lights and place wedding-color bows on some of the branches. Set pots of poinsettias in front of the trees and around the room. Hang glass or clear plastic snowflakes from the ceiling using fishing line.

❧ For an outdoor reception or an indoor reception with an outdoor feel, rent an arched trellis and decorate it with flowers, tulle, garlands, or twinkle lights. Set potted trees and colorful plants around the trellis; it'll make a beautiful backdrop for photos.

A note about twinkle lights

Unless one of your wedding colors is deep green, you may not be wild about the green wires that attach most twinkle lights. Camouflaging them is easy: Wrap the wires in ribbon, strips of fabric, electrical tape, white florist tape, or even crepe paper streamers and glue or tape them at the ends. For safety sake, wrap only the wires—not the sockets the bulbs sit in—and use cool-to-the-touch bulbs. Another option is to buy twinkle lights with white wires from a wedding-supply store or catalog. One drawback, though—the white ones don't go on sale for half price at after-Christmas sales.

Now get going!

When it comes to reception decorations, this chapter has barely scratched the surface. Use the ideas here as a spark to ignite your own imagination and ingenuity and create an atmosphere that is a beautiful reflection of you on your special day.

 *Chapter 9*

Tying Up the Loose Ends

This isn't the most glamorous chapter in this book, but it's definitely one of the most important. Here's where we get down to the nuts and bolts of planning your wedding reception: keeping food safe and clean, obtaining your supplies, and operating the equipment. Regardless of the plan you choose, you'll need this information.

Keeping food safe and clean

Nothing can turn a joyful celebration into a disaster of epic proportions faster than food poisoning. You don't want the 6 o'clock news to lead off with a story about 100 people who ended up in intensive care after eating at your reception. Keep your guests and their stomachs safe by asking your reception team to use common sense and the following guidelines when they're preparing and serving the food.

- Wash your hands! Stop germs from spreading by washing your hands often with warm water and soap while you're preparing your menu item.

- Keep your work space clean. Before you begin, sanitize your counters and tabletops with a mild bleach solution (bleach and hot water). Wipe down the surfaces frequently as you work.

- If you prepare your food item early and freeze it, be sure to use proper thawing procedures when you're ready to add the final touches. Don't leave it on the kitchen counter to thaw at room temperature. Instead, move it to the refrigerator about 24 hours before you need it.

- Be sure to carefully follow the instructions provided in the job descriptions and arrive at the reception site no earlier than is recommended unless adequate refrigeration or heating is available. Once the cold items—especially those containing mayonnaise—are placed on the buffet table, they need to be consumed within about three-and-a-half hours. The hot items can be eaten safely for up to one hour after the Sterno has burned out.

Obtaining the supplies

In all probability, you don't already own everything you'll need for self-catering your reception. Let's face it, not many of us have a punch fountain or place settings for 200 tucked away in the attic. Unless you know someone who does, you're going to have to take some time to round up your supplies.

Each reception plan contains a list of the nonfood items you'll need, most of which are available at your local rental store. Before you head for the store and plop down your credit card, do a little legwork that can save you some serious money.

Look at the list and see what you already have or have access to. Does your reception site supply the tables and chairs? Mark them off the list. Will Aunt Eunice let you use her candelabras? Can you borrow the office coffeemakers? Scratch out everything you can get free or very inexpensively from another source; hopefully, your list will dwindle considerably.

Most likely, you won't be able to line through the place settings (plates, utensils, glasses, cups, and saucers), especially if your guest list is large. It's still not time to head to the rental store. Have you considered using disposable dishes instead of renting real ones? If you haven't checked out disposable tableware lately, you might be surprised at the wide range of products that are available. In addition to plastic utensils in your choice of colors and clear glasses in a variety of shapes and sizes, wedding- and party-supply stores carry plastic-coated paper plates in a rainbow of colors. This type of plate works well for lightweight, dry menu items, but because they're fairly thin, you may want to use something more substantial if you're serving anything heavy or wet. However, these plates should be sturdy enough for all of the reception plans in this book *except* the Ultimate and Backyard Barbecue plans.

Heavy-duty disposable dishes are also available at party-supply stores and food-service distributors. You can choose plastic and Styrofoam plates from a variety of designs—solid or marbled, for example—and a range of sizes and shapes. Also available are clear plastic plates and bowls that look like cut glass or that appear to be engraved. When you get into some of the clear plastic styles, your price is going to escalate and may even be higher than renting real dishes. Before you drop the idea of using the clear plastic plates, however, realize that they may be worth the extra cost. Disposables are, well, disposable and will save your reception team the time and trouble of collecting, scraping, rinsing, and stacking the dishes at the end of the reception. In addition, they won't have to spend all of their time during the reception clearing dirty dishes away. Because they're graciously giving you their time and effort, you may want to consider spending a bit more money to make their job easier.

There's nothing wrong with mixing disposables and rented pieces. For example, you may decide that clear plastic plates and glasses will give you the elegant look you want and are worth the extra money for the time they'll save, but you just can't stomach that plastic flatware. Buy the dishes and rent the utensils. Even though your team will have to collect and rinse them, it's a lot easier than dealing with the entire place setting.

In addition to place settings, your supply list includes serving trays and bowls for many of the menu items. You can rent them, but remember that your reception team will need them ahead of time so they can prepare your food items. Unless you want to rent them early (and pay the extra fee for keeping them longer) or make day-before-the-wedding deliveries, look at your other options. One of the best of those options: Borrow, borrow, borrow!

Glass, silver, and white porcelain or china dishes don't have to be identical to look nice together on your serving tables. In fact, you can mix and match all three types of dishes on the same table and it'll look just fine. If your friends and family have trays that would work except for a spray of flowers or a group of dancing snowmen right smack in the middle, buy large doilies from a party-supply shop to cover up all but the outer rims. Not only will this disguise the offending ornamentation, but it will give your table a pulled-together look.

Another possibility: Check out the serving pieces available at party- and wedding-supply stores. They carry trays and bowls that look like they're made of silver or cut glass, but they're actually plastic—and covered in food, no one will ever know they're fakes. These serving pieces come in a variety of sizes and shapes and are reasonably priced.

For another serving tray option, visit the hardware store. Mirrors, mirrored tiles, and slabs of glass make delightfully different additions to your buffet table. Make your table setting even more interesting by placing a few glass blocks (also available at hardware stores) on the table first and setting clear glass slabs/trays on top. Be sure to get the edges of mirrors and glass slabs smoothed at the hardware store so no one will get cut if they brush up against them.

Going to the rental store

Take a look at your reception supplies list again. Once you've crossed off everything that you can borrow or get less expensively from another source, it's time to go to the rental store and place your order for whatever's left on the list.

Unless your uncle owns one, you may not know where to find a rental store. Check the Yellow Pages under Rentals or Rental Services. Get referrals from others who have used one and were happy with the service they received. If you live in a rural area or don't know of any in your town, contact the American Rental Association (1-800-334-2177; *www.ararental.org*); they can help you locate the stores closest to you.

Even if it's inconvenient or you'd rather spend your time doing something else, take the time to *go* to the store. Don't be tempted to place your order over the phone; meet with a real person who can show you around and personally help you with your needs. Your idea of beautiful china and high-quality linens may be completely different from a rental store clerk's idea, and you certainly don't want to find that out when your order is delivered on the day before the wedding.

A word of caution before you make your trip: Rental stores can seem like a little wonderland—all kinds of great gadgets, devices, and equipment that could make your reception the stuff of which legends are made. They carry everything from punch bowls and candelabras to waiters' trays and bread baskets to dance floors and portable bars. You could spend days in one, fantasizing about all the spectacular things you could do if you were to get one of these and two of those. To protect yourself from a severe case of impulse renting, be sure you know exactly what you need before you go to the store. You don't want to get home and realize that, even though it seemed like a really cool idea while you were in the store, that cotton candy machine you rented just doesn't have a place in your reception plans! Stick to your list and keep your pocketbook in mind so you don't find yourself way off track and over budget.

Deciding what you need to rent is the hard part; the rental process itself is simple and straightforward. Go to the store a month or two in advance (more, if your reception is during a peak wedding month) and reserve what you need. Seriously consider taking out the damage insurance most rental companies offer. The fee will kick your cost up by about 12 percent, but if anything is lost or broken, you won't have to pay for it. The standard rental period for weddings runs Friday (delivery day) through Monday (pick-up day). Make sure that the store delivers your order the day before the reception; if you've forgotten anything or the store makes a mistake in your order, you'll have time to fix things. Tell your reception team not to worry about washing dishes or linens before the pick-up date—the rental fee you're paying covers the cost of cleaning. However, rental company employees, especially those who have to pick up orders after functions are over, truly appreciate customers who scrape and/or rinse dishes and stack everything by a doorway for easier collection.

Reception equipment

The reception plan you choose may include foods that require more than just trays, bowls, and baskets for serving. Many rental companies provide instructions for the assembly and/or operation of any equipment they loan out, but some don't. In case your rental company is one of the latter, here's a quick how-to for chafing dishes and punch fountains, the only special equipment any of the reception plans require.

Chafing dishes

Chafing dishes typically have five parts: a frame, two Sterno holders with lids, a 4"-deep insert pan, a 2"-deep food pan, and a lid. When it's time to set up the reception hall, place the frame on the buffet table in its designated location (see your reception plan's buffet table diagram). Insert the Sterno holders into the holes in the bottom of the frame. Pop off the tops of the fuel cans and drop them into the holders. Place the holder lids on top of the holder and open them halfway. Pour about two quarts of water into the 4" insert pan, lower the pan into the frame, and light the Sterno with a match. (A 7-ounce can will burn for about three hours if it's half opened, two to two-and-a-half hours if it's wide open.) Pour your food into the 2" pan and lower it inside the 4" pan. Place the chafing lid on top.

Punch fountain

Place the fountain on the drink station table (see your plan's reception room diagram). Find the closest electrical outlet and plug it in. Unless the punch table is butted up against the wall right in front of the outlet, you may need an extension cord. If you have to run a cord across the floor, be sure to tape it down so your guests won't trip over it. Pour hot water into the fountain's large bowl, turn the switch on, and let water run through the fountain for about five minutes to make sure it's clean. Empty the water, place ice in the bowl, and pour the punch in until the bowl is full. Turn on the switch and the fountain will begin to flow. To fill glasses, hold them under the trickling streams of the fountain.

Some final words of wisdom

Organization and planning are key to catering your own wedding reception, but don't discount the value of flexibility and the ability to roll with the punches. If you get to the rental store, for example, and find that all of the punch fountains have already been rented, don't think your reception is doomed to be a pathetic flop. Rent a punchbowl instead or substitute iced tea for punch and serve it from a drink dispenser or pretty glass pitchers. Did you forget to order napkins engraved with your names until two days before the wedding? Don't worry about it; party-supply stores carry napkins in a rainbow of colors and no one will care that your names aren't plastered all over them.

The point is, it doesn't matter if you plan and organize your reception down to the most minute detail—something is going to go differently than the way you expect it to (you'll notice I didn't say "wrong"!). Just relax, improvise when you need to, and savor this very special time in your life.

 *Chapter 10*

Alternate Recipes

These recipes can be substituted for recipes in the reception plans. For best results, exchange like dishes. For example, if you are doing the Ultimate Reception and don't care for the cheeseball recipe in that plan, substitute with a cheeseball recipe from this chapter. If you take out the cheeseball and substitute something such as Tangy Chicken Wings or Seafood Stuffed Mushrooms, your menu will be out of balance.

Chili Cheeseballs

Number of guests	100	150	200
Monterey Jack cheese, grated	4½ cups	6¾ cups	8 cups
Fontina cheese, grated	1½ cups	2¼ cups	3 cups
Cream cheese, softened	8 oz	12 oz	16 oz
Dijon mustard	2 Tbsp.	3 Tbsp.	4 Tbsp.
Worcestershire sauce	2 tsp.	3 tsp.	4 tsp.
Garlic, minced	1¼ tsp.	1¾ tsp.	2½ tsp.
Chili powder	1 Tbsp.	1½ Tbsp.	2 Tbsp.
Parsley, chopped	1 cup	1½ cups	2 cups

Mix all ingredients (except for the parsley) in a large mixing bowl.

Shape into two balls and roll in the parsley. Wrap each cheeseball in plastic wrap and refrigerate until ready to build your trays.

Walnut Cheeseballs

Number of guests	100	150	200
Blue Cheese, fresh crumbles	1 lb.	1½ lbs.	2 lbs.
Butter, softened	1 lb.	1½ lbs.	2 lbs.
Walnuts, chopped	1 cup	1½ cups	2 cups
Heavy cream	4 Tbsp.	6 Tbsp.	8 Tbsp.
Almonds, ground	1 cup	1½ cups	2 cups

Mix all ingredients (except for the almonds) in a large mixing bowl.

Shape into two balls and roll in the almonds. Wrap each cheeseball in plastic wrap and refrigerate until ready to build the trays.

Firecracker Cheeseballs

Number of guests	100	150	200
Butter (softened)	½ lb.	¾ lb.	1 lb.
Cream cheese (softened)	1½ lbs.	2¼ lbs.	3 lbs.
Dry mustard	1 Tbsp.	1½ Tbsp.	2 Tbsp.
Curry powder	1½ tsp.	2 ¼ tsp.	3 tsp.
Worcestershire sauce	3 Tbsp.	4½ Tbsp.	6 Tbsp.
Tabasco sauce	2 tsp.	3 tsp.	4 tsp.
Soy sauce	1 Tbsp.	1½ Tbsp.	2 Tbsp.
Salt	1 tsp.	1½ tsp.	2 tsp.
Cayenne pepper	1 Tbsp.	1½ Tbsp.	2 Tbsp.
Doritos, crushed	1 cup	1½ cups	2 cups

Mix all ingredients (except for Doritos) in a large mixing bowl.

Shape into two balls and roll in Doritos. Wrap each cheeseball in plastic wrap and refrigerate until ready to build the trays.

Sweet and Tangy Chicken Wings

Number of guests	100	150	200
Chicken wings, fresh	22 lbs.	33 lbs.	44 lbs.
Seasoning salt	sprinkle	sprinkle	sprinkle
Light brown sugar, 1 lb. box	5	7½	10
All-purpose flour	1¼ cups	1¾ cups	2½ cups
Water	2½ cups	3¾ cups	5 cups
White vinegar	1¼ cups	1¾ cups	2½ cups
Soy sauce	1¼ cups	1¾ cups	2½ cups
Ketchup	5 Tbsp.	7½ Tbsp.	10 Tbsp.
Parsley	pinch	pinch	pinch

Place wings on a foil-lined sheet pan. Lightly sprinkle wings with seasoning salt. Bake in 350 degree oven for 30 minutes.

In a sauce pan, mix flour and sugar together. Add remaining ingredients and cook over medium heat until mixture begins to boil and thicken. Brush wings with sauce. Bake in oven for 35 minutes. Remove from oven, brush again with sauce and bake for 15 more minutes. Remove from oven and wrap tightly with foil wrap.

The chafing dishes will be at the reception site. Follow the chafing dish assembly instructions.

Seafood Stuffed Mushrooms

Number of guests	100	150	200
Cream cheese, softened, 8 oz. pack	4	6	8
Margarine, softened	2 cups	3 cups	4 cups
Horseradish, prepared	¼ cup	3/8 cup	½ cup
Garlic salt	4 tsp.	6 tsp.	8 tsp.
Canned shrimp, drained	1 lb.	1½ lbs.	2 lbs.
Canned crabmeat, drained	1 lb.	1½ lbs.	2 lbs.
Large mushrooms, fresh	100	150	200

In a large mixing bowl, combine cream cheese, margarine, horseradish, and garlic salt. Mix well until you have a smooth paste.

Add shrimp and crab to paste and mix thoroughly.

Remove stems from mushrooms.

Stuff mushrooms with seafood stuffing. Place mushrooms on baking sheets. Bake stuffed mushrooms in 350 degree oven for approximately 15 minutes.

The chafing dishes will be at the reception site. Follow the chafing dish assembly instructions.

Note: You may stuff the mushrooms one day before the reception, cover with plastic wrap, and keep refrigerated until ready to bake. After baking, transport immediately to the reception site.

Seafood-Stuffed Artichoke Bottoms

Number of guests	100	150	200
Artichoke bottoms, 8 ct. can	13	20	26
Mayonnaise, cold	2 cups	3 cups	4 cups
Sour cream, cold	1 cup	1½ cups	2 cups
Salt	2 tsp.	3 tsp.	4 tsp.
White ground pepper	1 tsp.	2 tsp.	3 tsp.
Melted butter, warm, not hot	3 sticks	4½ sticks	6 sticks
Frozen bay shrimp, thawed, drained.	1½ lbs.	2¼ lbs.	3 lbs
Frozen imitation crab, thawed, drained	2½ lbs.	3¾ lbs.	5 lbs.
Fresh celery, cold, ¼" diced	4 cups	6 cups	8 cups
Fresh green onion, ¼" diced	2 cups	3 cups	4 cups
20" trays, glass or silver	2	2	2
Tongs	4	6	8
Yield	7 lbs.	11 lbs.	14 lbs.

Whip mayonnaise, sour cream, salt, and white pepper together in a large mixing bowl. Slowly whip butter into mayonnaise mixture.

Using a rubber spatula, fold in the remaining ingredients. Gently toss until well blended. Do not overmix. Wrap tightly and refrigerate until ready to stuff artichokes.

Open the cans of artichoke bottoms and drain well. Place the artichokes on your trays face up. Stuff the artichokes with the seafood salad. Wrap the trays tightly with plastic wrap and refrigerate.

If you have extras, place them on a cookie sheet, cover with plastic wrap, and refrigerate. You'll use these to replenish the trays at the reception.

Seafood-Stuffed Cucumbers

Number of guests	100	150	200
Cucumbers	17	26	34
Mayonnaise, cold	2 cups	3 cups	4 cups
Sour cream, cold	1 cup	1½ cups	2 cups
Salt	2 tsp.	3 tsp.	4 tsp.
White ground pepper	1 tsp.	2 tsp.	3 tsp.
Melted butter, warm, not hot	3 sticks	4½ sticks	6 sticks
Frozen bay shrimp, thawed, drained	1½ lbs.	2¼ lbs.	3 lbs.
Frozen imitation crab, thawed, drained	2½ lbs.	3¾ lbs.	5 lbs.
Fresh celery, cold, ¼" diced	4 cups	6 cups	8 cups
Fresh green onion, ¼" diced	2 cups	3 cups	4 cups
20" trays, glass or silver	2	2	2
Yield	7 lbs.	11 lbs.	14 lbs.

Whip mayonnaise, sour cream, salt, and white pepper together in a large mixing bowl. Slowly whip butter into mayonnaise mixture.

Using a rubber spatula, fold in the remaining ingredients. Gently toss until well blended. Do not overmix. Wrap tightly and refrigerate until ready to stuff the cucumbers.

Cut the ends off a cucumber (about ½"). Cut the cucumber in half lengthwise. Cut each half into 3 equal parts. You should have 6 equal parts per cucumber.

Hollow out the inner core leaving about ¼" intact on each end.

Stuff the cucumber boat with seafood salad and arrange on trays. Wrap tightly with plastic wrap and refrigerate.

If you have extras, place them on a cookie sheet, cover with plastic wrap, and refrigerate. You'll use these to replenish the trays at the reception.

Hearts of Palm Rollups

Number of guests	100	150	200
Smoked ham, 2 oz. slices	18 lbs.	27 lbs.	36 lbs.
Hearts of palm	144	216	288
Vinegar	½ cup	¾ cup	1 cup
Lemon juice	2½ Tbsp.	3¾ Tbsp.	5 Tbsp.
Olive oil	1 pt.	1 ½ pts.	2 pts.
Salt	1 tsp.	1½ tsp.	2 tsp.
Pepper	1 tsp.	1½ tsp.	2 tsp.
Dried basil	1 Tbsp.	1½ Tbsp.	2 Tbsp.
Anchovy fillets	16	24	32
Whipping cream	1 pt.	1½ pts.	2 pts.
Mayonnaise	2¾ cups	4¼ cups	8¼ cups
Stuffed olives	144	216	288
Frilly toothpicks	144	216	288
20" round tray, glass or silver	2	3	4
Glass bowls	2	3	4
Small serving spoons	4	6	8

This dish may be prepared the day before the reception.

Drain the hearts of palm, pour onto paper towels, and pat dry.

Whip the vinegar, lemon juice, oil, salt, and pepper together. Finely dice anchovy fillets, mix with basil, and add to oil mixture. Whip well.

Place hearts of palm in a large, shallow dish and pour in the marinade. Marinate covered for two hours at room temperature.

Lay out ham slices on a sanitized counter top.

Drain the hearts of palm from the marinade and place one heart of palm on top of a ham slice. Roll the heart of palm up in the ham. Stick an olive on a frilly toothpick and insert into the middle of the rollup. Place the prepared rollups onto your trays, leaving space in the center for the dip.

Whip the mayonnaise and whipping cream together. Pour into glass bowls. Place bowls of dip in the center of the trays.

Wrap the prepared trays with plastic wrap and refrigerate.

Barbecue Pork Spareribs

Number of guests	25	50	75
Ketchup	3 cups	4½ cups	6 cups
Orange juice	3 cups	4½ cups	6 cups
Honey	1 cup	1½ cups	2 cups
Soy sauce	½ cup	¾ cup	1 cup
Garlic cloves (chopped fine)	6	9	12
Salt	1 Tbsp.	1½ Tbsp.	2 Tbsp.
Pepper	2 tsp.	3 tsp.	4 tsp.
Pork spareribs	25 lbs.	50 lbs.	75 lbs.
Serving trays	2	4	6
Tongs	4	8	12

In a large bowl, combine all ingredients except the spareribs. Mix well.

With a large knife, cut spareribs into two-bone portions.

Place the ribs in large, shallow pans and pour the marinade over them. Cover the pans with foil and marinate in the refrigerator overnight.

Preheat grill to 300 degrees. Place the ribs on the grill and cook slowly—away from high heat to avoid burning—for approximately 1½ hours or until meat pulls freely from the bone. Baste often during cooking with the remaining marinade. If grills aren't available, the ribs may be cooked in a 300 degree oven for 1½ hours.

Serve hot off the grill.

Bruncheon Eggs

Number of guests	25	50	75
Canadian bacon slices	36	72	108
Swiss cheese slices, 1 oz	36	72	108
Eggs	36	72	108
Whipping cream	3 cups	6 cups	10 cups
Grated parmesan cheese	1 cup	2 cups	3 cups
Black pepper	1 tsp.	2 tsp.	1 Tbsp.
Paprika	sprinkle	sprinkle	sprinkle
Chopped parsley	sprinkle	sprinkle	sprinkle
13" x 9" x 2" baking dish	3	6	9
Serving spoons	3	6	9

Line the bottom of lightly greased baking dishes with Canadian bacon. Top with Swiss cheese slices.

Break eggs (whole) into the baking dishes and space them apart evenly. Pour whipping cream over eggs.

Bake at 425 degrees for 12 minutes.

Sprinkle with parmesan cheese, pepper, and paprika. Return dishes to oven for an additional 12 minutes or until set.

Sprinkle with parsley. Let set at room temperature for 10 minutes before serving.

Marinated Shrimp

Number of guests	100	150	200
Shrimp, cooked, peeled, deveined, tail removed	20 lbs.	30 lbs.	40 lbs.
Lemons, sliced thin	20	20	20
Large red onions, sliced thin	4	4	4
Olive oil	13 cups	19 cups	26 cups
Tarragon vinegar	7 cups	11 cups	14 cups
Lemon juice	½ cup	¾ cup	1 cup
Salt	½ cup	¾ cup	1 cup
Pepper	¼ cup	1/3 cup	½ cup
Glass punch bowls	2	2	2
Small tongs	4	4	4

Make this recipe the day before the reception.

Line the glass punch bowls with onion slices, covering the entire inner surface. Place sliced lemons on top of the onion slices, covering the entire inner surface. Place shrimp in bowls.

Combine olive oil, vinegar, lemon juice, salt, and pepper in a container with a lid. Shake well until completely mixed.

Pour marinade over shrimp. Toss the shrimp in the marinade, being careful not to disturb the sliced lemons and onions. Cover with plastic wrap and marinate overnight.

Next day, toss shrimp again.

Re-cover with plastic wrap and refrigerate.

The following recipes can be used for the sandwiches in the Basic Reception Plan if you prefer homemade over store-bought salads.

Chicken Salad

Number of guests	100	150	200
Mayonnaise	10 cups	15 cups	20 cups
Sweet pickle relish	2 cups	3 cups	4 cups
Salt	2 Tbsp.	3 Tbsp.	4 Tbsp.
White pepper	2 tsp.	3 tsp.	4 tsp.
Tarragon vinegar	1 Tbsp.	1.5 Tbsp.	2 Tbsp.
Worcestershire sauce	2 Tbsp.	3 Tbsp.	4 Tbsp.
White chicken meat, cooked and diced	10 lbs.	15 lbs.	20 lbs.
Hard-boiled eggs, chopped	8	12	16
Green onion, finely chopped	2 cups	3 cups	4 cups
Celery, finely chopped	4 cups	6 cups	8 cups

Place the first six ingredients in a large mixing bowl and whip until mixture is creamy and smooth.

In a separate bowl, mix the remaining four ingredients together. Pour the mayonnaise mixture into the chicken mixture and toss well. Do not overmix.

Cover tightly with plastic wrap and refrigerate.

Tuna Salad

Number of guests	100	150	200
Chunk light tuna, 12 oz can	14	21	28
Sliced green olives, 16 oz jar	4	6	8
Pickled cocktail onions, 12 oz jar	2	3	4
Diced beets, 8¼ oz can	2	3	4
Mayonnaise	3 cups	41/2 cups	6 cups
Sour cream	6 cups	9 cups	12 cups
Salt	3 tsp.	41/2 tsp.	6 tsp.
Paprika	6 tsp.	9 tsp.	12 tsp.
Tomato paste	12 Tbsp.	18 Tbsp.	24 Tbsp.
Hard-boiled eggs, chopped	12	18	24
Dill	4 Tbsp.	6 Tbsp.	8 Tbsp.

Open the cans of tuna and drain well. Place tuna in a large mixing bowl and flake apart using a fork.

Open and drain the olives, onions, and beets. Add to the tuna mixture.

In a separate bowl, whip the mayonnaise, sour cream, salt, paprika, tomato paste, and dill together. Pour this mixture into the tuna mixture.

Add eggs and toss well.

Cover with plastic wrap and refrigerate.

Ham Salad

Number of guests	100	150	200
Cooked ham, diced	6 lbs.	9 lbs.	12 lbs.
Red delicious apples, diced	14	21	28
Bananas, diced	14	21	28
Lemon juice	½ cup	¾ cup	1 cup
Mayonnaise	3 cups	4½ cups	6 cups
Whipping cream	2 cups	3 cups	4 cups
Lemon pepper	8 Tbsp.	12 Tbsp.	16 Tbsp.
Salt	1 Tbsp.	1½ Tbsp.	2 Tbsp.
Sugar	1 Tbsp.	1½ Tbsp.	2 Tbsp.

Dice ham, apples, and bananas into pea-sized pieces and toss together in a large bowl. Add lemon juice and toss well.

In a separate bowl, whip mayonnaise, whipping cream, lemon pepper, salt, and sugar together.

Add mayonnaise mixture to the ham and fruit mixture and toss well.

Cover tightly with plastic wrap and refrigerate.

 *Chapter 11*

Rehearsal Dinners

The Hawaiian Luau Rehearsal Dinner

The wedding rehearsal dinner. It's the much-overlooked, often dreaded (*What? I have to wear pantyhose again?*) formality in the grand production that is the wedding celebration. And there's often good reason for the dread. The last hurdle before the wedding day, the rehearsal dinner tends to feel like an afterthought or one of those obligations you just have to buck up and deal with: crowded restaurant, overwhelmed bride and groom, stressed-out in-laws, and more often than not, a server with the IQ of a goat.

Wouldn't it be great to have *one* event among all the pre-wedding festivities that people really look forward to? An event where the bride and groom can relax and spend time with their close friends and family without having to talk over the drunks at the next table or speed through supper so the restaurant can cycle more customers through? An event that meshes a time-honored wedding tradition with—gasp!—fun?

Well, here it is! With the Hawaiian Luau Rehearsal Dinner, you can almost feel the sand between your toes and the warm tropical breezes in your face. The luau features a wide variety of salads, entrees, and side dishes with a tropical flair, so even the pickiest eaters will find something they like. Serve everything in the plan or pick and choose the dishes you like best.

Depending on the number of items you decide to serve, you'll need up to 13 reliable friends to help you pull the Hawaiian Luau Rehearsal Dinner together. Most items in this plan can be assembled ahead of time, but even those that have to be made the day of the dinner are so simple, your helpers will have plenty of time to cook *and* limber up for the hukilau!

The Menu

Tropical Chicken Salad
Overnight Hawaiian Slaw
Pacific Potato Salad
Big Island Chicken
Mainland Seafood Lasagna
Hot Hawaiian Rice
Stir-Fried Vegetable Medley
Maui Lemon Bread
Pineapple Macadamia Nut Bread
Frozen Coconut Caramel Pie
Sparkling Luau Punch

The Helpers

You'll need up to 13 people to help with this reception. Detailed job descriptions for each team are provided later in this chapter, but here's a quick summary of the type of help you're looking for.

Set Up/Take Down Team: Get a couple of your brawny friends or family members to help you set up your rehearsal dinner site. They'll need to be able to haul tables and chairs, lay out the linens, and set the tables with place settings and centerpieces.

Tropical Chicken Salad Helper: Very little cooking but lots of chopping is required for this job. This salad is made the day before the rehearsal dinner, so be sure this helper has plenty of room in the refrigerator to store it overnight.

Overnight Hawaiian Slaw Helper: Another job that requires a lot of chopping. The only other culinary skill that this helper needs to possess is the ability to boil water (well, vinegar, actually)! This salad is made the day before the rehearsal dinner, so be sure your helper has plenty of room in the refrigerator to store it overnight.

Pacific Potato Salad Helper: Peeling and cooking potatoes is about as complicated as this one gets. Another day-before salad, so be sure your helper has plenty of room in the refrigerator to store it overnight.

Big Island Chicken Helper: This helper should know his or her way around a kitchen, but the dish is still very simple to prepare. It's made the morning of the rehearsal dinner and baked right before the helper walks out the door.

Mainland Seafood Lasagna Helper: Minimal cooking ability is required to prepare this dish. A little boiling, a little chopping, a little layering, and viola!—a great-tasting and very impressive entrée.

Hot Hawaiian Rice Helper: It's pretty tough to mess rice up, even when it's got a few extra ingredients added to it. This dish doesn't require any special skills (stirring doesn't count) to prepare.

Stir-fried Vegetable Medley Helper: Another dish that requires chopping, chopping, and more chopping. Cooking time is only about five minutes, so this one can be made the day of the dinner.

Maui Lemon Bread Helper: Give this job to your buddy who likes to bake. It's a simple bread—no rising or kneading required.

Pineapple Macadamia Nut Bread Helper: Another easy bread that's short on effort but long on taste. Turning on the mixer is the most difficult thing this helper will have to do.

Frozen Coconut Caramel Pie Helper: Here's a job for your friend who loves being in the spotlight because all of your guests will bow at his or her feet after the first bite of this delicious dessert! This pie requires overnight freezing, so make sure there's enough freezer space available.

Sparkling Luau Punch Helper: Does it get any easier than this? Mix up a bunch of liquids and turn on the punch fountain. This helper does need to possess a bit of heft, though, to lift five-gallon buckets of juice and pour them into the fountain.

The Hardware

In addition to recruiting the people who will help you with your reception, you'll need to rent or purchase the following items. Before whipping out your credit card, however, ask your rehearsal dinner site representative if they can provide any of the items free of charge or at a discount. You may also be able to borrow many of the items from friends and family members and save yourself some serious money. See Chapter Eight for complete information on renting or otherwise acquiring the supplies below.

Included in this list are white table linens and basic floral centerpieces. These are staples at traditional rehearsal dinners, but you may want to use some other type of decorations. Chapter Nine is packed with a huge variety of decorating ideas you may want to consider.

Number of guests:	25	50	75
12" dinner plates	25	50	75
Knives	25	50	75
Forks	25	50	75
Spoons	25	50	75
8" dessert plates	25	50	75
12oz. cups	25	50	75
20" x 20" white napkins	25	50	75
3-gallon punch fountain	1	1	1
Chairs	25	50	75
8' x 30" banquet tables	7	5	13
52" x 108" white tablecloths	7	5	13
60" round tables	0	5	0
90" round white tablecloths	0	5	0
21' white table skirts	3	3	3

NOTE: *Skirts are for the Buffet Table and Punch Table*

	25	50	75
Salt and pepper shakers	4 sets	7 sets	10 sets
Large centerpiece (buffet and head table)	2	2	2
Small centerpieces (dining tables and punch table)	6	9	12

Rehearsal Dinner Team Job Descriptions

Team 1: Set Up/Take Down Team

Helper #1 _____

Helper #2 _____

Rehearsal Dinner Coordinator _____

Rehearsal Dinner Location _____

Time of Dinner _____

Number of Guests _____

Responsibilities

- Arrive at dinner site three hours prior to dinner.
- Arrange tables and chairs using the Luau Dining Room diagram on pages 229–231.
- Place tablecloths on tables and attach skirting to buffet table and punch table.
- Set the dining tables with forks, knives, spoons, napkins, salt and pepper shakers, and centerpieces using the Luau Dining Room diagram on page 229–231 and the Luau Place Setting diagram on page 231.
- Set up punch table using the Luau Punch Table diagram on page 232.
- Place dinner plates on buffet table using the Luau Buffet diagram on page 232.
- Assist with clean up at the conclusion of dinner.

Team 2: Tropical Chicken Salad

Helper #1 _____

Rehearsal Dinner Coordinator _____

Rehearsal Dinner Location _____

Time of Dinner _____

Number of Guests _____

Responsibilities

❧ On the day before the rehearsal dinner, prepare the chicken salad according to the directions that follow. Because this salad requires refrigeration, you might want to clean out your refrigerator so that you have ample space to store it overnight.

❧ Arrive at the dinner site no earlier than 30 minutes prior to dinner. Place the bowl(s) of chicken salad and the serving spoons on the buffet table as shown on the Luau Buffet Table diagram on page 232.

❧ At the conclusion of dinner, assist with clean up.

Shopping List

Number of guests:	25	50	75
Large salad bowls	1	2	2
Serving spoons	2	4	4
Cooked chicken, diced	10 cups	20 cups	30 cups
Salad oil	¼ cup	½ cup	¾ cup
Orange juice	¼ cup	½ cup	¾ cup
Vinegar	¼ cup	½ cup	¾ cup
Salt	2 tsp.	4 tsp.	6 tsp.
Cooked rice	6 cups	12 cups	18 cups
Green grapes	3 cups	6 cups	9 cups
Celery, diced	3 cups	6 cups	9 cups
Pineapple tidbits (13½ oz. can) drained	2 cans	4 cans	6 cans
Mandarin oranges (11oz. can), drained	2 cans	4 cans	6 cans
Slivered almonds, toasted	2 cups	4 cups	6 cups
Mayonnaise	3 cups	6 cups	9 cups

Tropical Chicken Salad

Combine all ingredients and toss well.

Cover with film wrap and refrigerate overnight.

Team 3: Overnight Hawaiian Slaw

Helper #1 _____

Rehearsal Dinner Coordinator _____

Rehearsal Dinner Location _____

Time of Dinner _____

Number of Guests _____

Responsibilities

⚘ On the day before the rehearsal dinner, prepare the slaw according to the directions on page 216. Because this dish requires refrigeration, you might want to clean out your refrigerator so that you have ample space to store it overnight.

⚘ Arrive at the dinner site no earlier than 30 minutes prior to dinner and place the bowl(s) of slaw and the serving spoons on the buffet table as shown on the Luau Buffet Table diagram on page 232.

⚘ At the conclusion of dinner, assist with clean up.

Shopping List

Number of guests:	25	50	75
Large bowls	1	2	2
Large serving spoons	2	4	4
Green cabbage, shredded	2 heads	4 heads	6 heads
Red onions (medium), thinly sliced	2	4	6
Red pepper, diced	1 cup	2 cups	3 cups
Green pepper, diced	1 cup	2 cups	3 cups
Green olives, stuffed	1 cup	2 cups	3 cups
White vinegar	1 cup	2 cups	3 cups
Vegetable oil	1 cup	2 cups	3 cups
Sugar	1 cup	2 cups	3 cups
Dijon mustard	1½ Tbsp.	3 Tbsp.	4½ Tbsp.

Overnight Hawaiian Slaw

In a large bowl, combine cabbage, onion, peppers, and green olives.

In a saucepan, combine vinegar, oil, sugar, and Dijon mustard; bring to boil and cook for one minute. Remove from heat and allow to cool for 30 minutes. Pour over vegetables and mix well.

Wrap with film wrap and refrigerate overnight.

Mix again prior to serving.

Team 4: Pacific Potato Salad Team

Helper #1 _____

Rehearsal Dinner Coordinator _____

Rehearsal Dinner Location _____

Time of Dinner _____

Number of Guests _____

Responsibilities

❦ On the day before the rehearsal dinner, prepare the potato salad according to the directions on page 217. Because this dish requires refrigeration, you might want to clean out your refrigerator so that you have ample space to store it overnight.

❦ Arrive at the dinner site no earlier than 30 minutes prior to dinner and place the bowl(s) of potato salad and the serving spoons on the buffet table as shown on the Luau Buffet Table diagram on page 232.

❦ At the conclusion of dinner, assist with clean up.

Shopping List

Number of guests:	25	50	75
Large bowls	1	2	2
Large serving spoons	2	4	4
Small new potatoes	6 lbs.	12 lbs.	18 lbs.
Hard-cooked eggs, chopped	6	12	18
Apples, chopped	2 ¼ cups	4 ½ cups	6 ¾ cups
Green grapes, halved	2 ¼ cups	4 ½ cups	6 ¾ cups
Onion, chopped	¾ cup	1 ½ cups	2 ¼ cups
Green pepper, chopped	¾ cup	1 ½ cups	2 ¼ cups
Mayonnaise	1 ½ cups	3 cups	4 ½ cups
Lemon juice	6 Tbsp.	12 Tbsp.	18 Tbsp.
Salt	¾ tsp.	1 ½ tsp.	2 ¼ tsp.
White pepper	¼ tsp.	½ tsp.	¾ tsp.

Pacific Potato Salad

Cook potatoes in boiling water for 25 minutes or until tender. Drain and allow to cool.

Peel potatoes and cut into ½" thick slices.

Place potato slices in a large mixing bowl and add eggs, apples, grapes, onion, and green pepper. Toss gently.

In a separate bowl, mix together mayonnaise, lemon juice, salt, and pepper.

Pour mayonnaise mixture over potato mixture and lightly toss just until coated.

Wrap with film wrap and refrigerate overnight.

Team 5: Big Island Chicken

Helper #1 _____

Rehearsal Dinner Coordinator _____

Rehearsal Dinner Location _____

Time of Dinner _____

Number of Guests _____

Responsibilities

❧ On the morning of the rehearsal dinner, prepare the Big Island Chicken according to the directions that follow. Cover and refrigerate until ready to bake.

❧ This item needs approximately 45 minutes cooking time; so allow yourself enough time to travel to the dinner site after baking.

❧ Arrive at the dinner site no earlier than 30 minutes prior to dinner and place the chicken and serving spoons on the buffet table as shown on the Luau Buffet Table diagram on page 232.

❧ At the conclusion of dinner, assist with clean up.

Shopping List

Number of guests:	25	50	75
Casserole dishes (9" x 13" x 2")	4	8	12
Large serving spoons	4	8	12
Boneless, skinless chicken breasts	12 lbs.	24 lbs.	36 lbs.
Margarine	½ cup	1 cup	1½ cups
Coco Lopez (Cream of Coconut)	3 cups	6 cups	9 cups
ReaLime (lime juice from concentrate)	1 cup	2 cups	3 cups
Soy sauce	¼ cup	½ cup	¾ cup
Cornstarch	1 tsp.	2 tsp.	3 tsp.
Red bell pepper, diced	2 cups	4 cups	6 cups
Green bell pepper, diced	2 cups	4 cups	6 cups
Pineapple chunks	4 cups	8 cups	12 cups
Onions, sliced thick	4	8	12

Big Island Chicken

Preheat oven to 350 degrees.

Cut chicken breasts into 1" cubes. Brown chicken cubes in margarine; drain. Distribute chicken evenly in baking dishes.

Dissolve cornstarch in soy sauce. Pour into the skillet used to brown the chicken. Add Cream of Coconut and ReaLime. Bring to a boil and reduce heat.

Add remaining ingredients and simmer for five minutes. Pour evenly over chicken and bake uncovered for 45 minutes.

Team 6: Mainland Seafood Lasagna

Helper #1 _____

Rehearsal Dinner Coordinator _____

Rehearsal Dinner Location _____

Time of Dinner _____

Number of Guests _____

Responsibilities

❧ On the day before the rehearsal dinner, prepare (but do not bake) the lasagna according to the directions on page 220. Refrigerate and cook on day of rehearsal dinner.

❧ This item needs approximately 45 minutes cooking time; so allow yourself enough time to travel to the dinner site after baking.

❧ Arrive at the dinner site no earlier than 30 minutes prior to dinner and place the lasagna and serving spoons on the buffet table as shown on the Luau Buffet Table diagram on page 232.

❧ At the conclusion of dinner, assist with clean up.

Shopping List

Number of guests:	25	50	75
Casserole dishes (9" x 13" x 2")	2	4	6
Large serving spoons	4	8	12
Lasagna noodles	16	32	48
Margarine	¼ cup	½ cup	¾ cup
Onion, chopped	2 cups	4 cups	6 cups
Cream cheese, softened	16 oz.	32 oz.	48 oz.
Cottage cheese	3 cups	6 cups	9 cups
Eggs, beaten	2	4	6
Basil	4 tsp.	8 tsp.	12 tsp.
Salt	1 tsp.	2 tsp.	1 Tbsp.
Pepper	¼ tsp.	½ tsp.	¾ tsp.
Cream of mushroom soup, 10 ½ oz.	4	8	12
Milk	2/3 cup	1¼ cups	2 cups
White wine	2/3 cup	1¼ cups	2 cups
Crabmeat, 5oz. can	2 cans	4 cans	6 cans
Cooked shrimp, peeled	2 lbs.	4 lbs.	6 lbs.
Parmesan cheese, grated	½ cup	1 cup	1½ cups
Cheddar cheese, shredded	1 cup	2 cups	3 cups

Mainland Seafood Lasagna

Cook noodles according to package directions; drain. Distribute evenly in 9" x 13" pans.

Sauté onion in margarine. In a bowl, combine onions, cream cheese, cottage cheese, eggs, basil, salt and pepper; mix well. Spread half of mixture over noodles.

In a bowl, combine soup, milk and wine and mix well. Stir in crab and shrimp. Spoon half of mixture over cheese layer.

Repeat all layers. Sprinkle with Parmesan cheese.

Cover with foil and place in refrigerator until ready to bake.

Bake covered at 350 degrees for 45 minutes. Top with cheddar cheese, brown under broiler. Let stand 20 minutes before serving.

Team 7: Hot Hawaiian Rice

Helper #1 _____

Rehearsal Dinner Coordinator _____

Rehearsal Dinner Location _____

Time of Dinner _____

Number of Guests _____

Responsibilities

- On the morning of the rehearsal dinner, prepare the rice according to the directions on page 221. Cover and refrigerate until ready to bake.

- This item needs approximately one hour and 10 minutes of cooking time, so allow yourself enough time to travel to the dinner site after baking.

- Arrive at the dinner site no earlier than 30 minutes prior to dinner and place the rice and serving spoons on the buffet table as shown on the Luau Buffet Table diagram on page 232.

- At the conclusion of dinner, assist with clean up.

Shopping List

Number of guests:	25	50	75
3 qt. baking dishes	2	4	6
Serving spoons	2	4	6
Uncooked brown rice	5 cups	10 cups	15 cups
Crushed pineapple, drained (reserve juice)	2 cups	4 cups	6 cups
Raisins	2 cups	4 cups	6 cups
Large apples, peeled and cubed	2	4	6
Small onion, coarsely chopped	4	8	12
Sliced water chestnuts, 8 oz. can	4	8	12
Celery, diced	4 stalks	8 stalks	12 stalks
Red pepper flakes	1 tsp.	2 tsp.	3 tsp.
Apple juice concentrate	¼ cup	½ cup	¾ cup
Turmeric	1 tsp.	2 tsp.	3 tsp.
Reserved pineapple juice plus water to equal:	2 ½ qts.	5 qts.	7 ½ qts.
Soy sauce	4 Tbsp.	8 Tbsp.	12 Tbsp.

Hot Hawaiian Rice

Divide rice evenly among the baking dishes.

In a bowl, mix together the crushed pineapple, raisins, apples, onion, water chestnuts, celery, and red pepper flakes. Distribute evenly on top of rice.

In a bowl, combine the apple juice concentrate, turmeric, pineapple juice, water, and soy sauce; mix well. Pour liquid mixture evenly over rice mixture and stir well.

Cover with foil and bake at 325 degrees for 1 hour and 10 minutes. Check for doneness.

Team 8: Stir-fried Vegetable Medley

Helper #1 _____

Rehearsal Dinner Coordinator _____

Rehearsal Dinner Location _____

Time of Dinner _____

Number of Guests _____

Responsibilities

 Two hours prior to the rehearsal dinner, prepare the stir-fried vegetables according to the directions that follow.

 Arrive at the dinner site no earlier than 30 minutes prior to dinner and place the stir-fried vegetables and tongs on the buffet table as shown on the Luau Buffet Table diagram on page 232.

 At the conclusion of dinner, assist with clean up.

Shopping List

Number of guests:	25	50	75
Serving bowl	1	2	2
Serving tongs	2	4	4
Vegetable oil	¾ cup	1 ½ cups	2 ¼ cups
Cabbage, coarsely shredded	3 heads	6 heads	9 heads
Red onion (medium), sliced	3	6	9
Large carrots, thinly sliced	4	8	12
Tomatoes, cut into wedges	5	10	15
Fresh dill, minced	4 Tbsp.	8 Tbsp.	12 Tbsp.
Salt	1 tsp.	2 tsp.	3 tsp.
Cracked black pepper	1 tsp.	2 tsp.	3 tsp.

Stir-Fried Vegetable Medley

Pour oil into a large preheated 325-degree wok or skillet, and allow oil to get hot. Add vegetables and stir-fry for three minutes. Add remaining ingredients and stir-fry for one minute.

Transfer vegetables to serving bowls and cover with foil to keep warm until ready to transport to rehearsal dinner site.

Team 9: Maui Lemon Bread

Helper #1 _____

Rehearsal Dinner Coordinator _____

Rehearsal Dinner Location _____

Time of Dinner _____

Number of Guests _____

Responsibilities

- On the morning of the rehearsal dinner, prepare the lemon bread according to the directions on page 224.

- Arrive at the dinner site no earlier than 30 minutes prior to dinner and place the baskets of lemon bread and the tongs on the buffet table as shown on the Luau Buffet Table diagram on page 232.

- At the conclusion of dinner, assist with clean up.

Shopping List

Number of guests:	25	50	75
Bread basket w/napkin	1	2	3
Serving tongs	2	4	6
Loaf pans (8.5" x 4.5" x 3")	2	4	6
Margarine	½ cup	1 cup	1½ cups
Sugar	1½ cups	3 cups	4½ cups
Eggs, lightly beaten	4	8	12
Lemon rinds, grated	2 lemons	4 lemons	6 lemons
All-purpose flour, sifted	4 cups	8 cups	12 cups
Baking powder	5 tsp.	10 tsp.	15 tsp.
Salt	2 tsp.	4 tsp.	6 tsp.
Milk	1½ cups	3 cups	4½ cups
Walnuts, chopped	1 cup	2 cups	3 cups
Lemon juice	2 Tbsp.	4 Tbsp.	6 Tbsp.
Sugar	4 Tbsp.	8 Tbsp.	12 Tbsp.

Maui Lemon Bread

In a large mixing bowl, cream together the margarine and sugar until light and fluffy. Add eggs and lemon rind and mix well.

In a separate bowl, sift together flour, baking powder, and salt. Add to mixture alternately with milk, beginning and ending with sifted ingredients.

Stir in walnuts.

Pour evenly into greased loaf pans.

Bake at 350 degrees for 55 minutes to an hour or until bread passes the toothpick test.

In a small bowl, combine lemon juice and sugar and spoon over bread immediately after removing from the oven.

Allow bread to cool. Remove from pans and slice thin.

Place sliced bread in napkin-lined bread basket(s).

Serve at room temperature.

Team 10: Pineapple Macadamia Nut Bread

Helper #1 _____

Rehearsal Dinner Coordinator _____

Rehearsal Dinner Location _____

Time of Dinner _____

Number of Guests _____

Responsibilities

- On the morning of the rehearsal dinner, prepare Pineapple Macadamia Nut Bread according to the directions on page 225.

- Arrive at the dinner site no earlier than 30 minutes prior to dinner and place the baskets of bread and the tongs on the buffet table as shown on the Luau Buffet Table diagram on page 232.

- At the conclusion of dinner, assist with clean up.

Shopping List

Number of guests:	25	50	75
Bread basket w/napkin	1	2	3
Serving tongs	2	4	6
Loaf pans (8.5" x 4.5" x 3")	2	4	6
Butter, softened	½ cup	1 cup	1½ cups
Light brown sugar	1½ cups	3 cups	4½ cups
Eggs, lightly beaten	4	8	12
All-purpose flour, sifted	3 ½ cups	7 cups	10 ½ cups
Baking powder	4 tsp.	8 tsp.	12 tsp.
Baking soda	½ tsp.	1 tsp.	1 ½ tsp.
Salt	1 tsp.	2 tsp.	3 tsp.
Macadamia nuts, chopped	1 ½ cups	3 cups	4 ½ cups
Fresh pineapple, shredded	2 cups	4 cups	6 cups

Pineapple Macadamia Nut Bread

In a large mixing bowl, cream together the butter and sugar until light and fluffy. Add eggs and mix well.

In a separate bowl, combine flour, baking powder, baking soda, and salt. Add nuts and mix well.

Stir half of the flour mixture into the creamed mixture.

Add pineapple and remaining flour mixture.

Pour batter evenly into greased loaf pans.

Bake at 350 degrees for 1 hour or until bread passes the toothpick test.

Allow bread to cool.

Remove from pans and slice thin.

Place sliced bread in napkin-lined bread basket(s).

Serve at room temperature.

Team 11: Frozen Coconut Caramel Pie

Helper #1 _____

Rehearsal Dinner Coordinator _____

Rehearsal Dinner Location _____

Time of Dinner _____

Number of Guests _____

Responsibilities

- One day before the rehearsal dinner, prepare the coconut caramel pies according to the directions on page 227. Wrap and freeze overnight.

- On the day of the dinner, slice the pies and return to freezer.

- Arrive at the site no earlier than 30 minutes prior to the time of dinner. Pre-plate and set the desserts at each place setting above the napkin. Dessert plates will be provided for you at the site. The punch helper can help you plate up and set out the desserts when their job is completed.

- At the conclusion of dinner, assist with clean up.

Shopping List

Number of guests:	25	50	75
Baking dishes (13" x 9" x 2")	2	4	6
Pie spatulas	1	2	2
Self-rising flour	3 cups	6 cups	9 cups
Margarine, softened	1½ cups	3 cups	4½ cups
Pecans, chopped	1½ cups	3 cups	4½ cups
Margarine	½ cup	1 cup	1½ cups
Flaked coconut, 7 oz. can	2	4	6
Pecans, chopped	1 cup	2 cups	3 cups
Cream cheese, softened	16 oz.	32 oz.	48 oz.
Sweetened condensed milk, 14 oz. can	2	4	6
Cool Whip, thawed	24 oz.	48 oz.	72 oz.
Caramel sauce, 12 oz. jar	2	4	6

Frozen Coconut Caramel Pie

Combine the first three ingredients and press firmly into lightly-greased baking dishes.

Bake at 350 degrees for 16 to 20 minutes or until lightly browned. Remove from oven and allow to cool.

Using a saucepan, melt butter; add coconut and chopped pecans. Cook over low heat until coconut is light brown. Remove from heat and allow to cool.

Using an electric mixer, beat the cream cheese and sweetened condensed milk until smooth. Fold in Cool Whip.

Layer one third each of cream cheese mixture, caramel sauce, and coconut mixture over crust.

Repeat layers twice. Cover dessert, and freeze overnight.

Cutting instructions: Each pan will yield 15 square desserts when cutting a 3 x 5 grid.

Team 12: Sparkling Luau Punch

Helper #1 _____

Rehearsal Dinner Coordinator _____

Rehearsal Dinner Location _____

Time of Dinner _____

Number of Guests _____

Responsibilities

- On the morning of the rehearsal dinner, partially prepare the punch according to the instructions on page 228.

- Arrive at the site no earlier than 30 minutes prior to the time of dinner and complete preparation of the punch

- Help dessert person plate up and set desserts at each place setting above the napkin.

- At the conclusion of the dinner, assist with clean up.

Shopping List

Number of guests:	25	50	75
Five-gallon bucket	1	1	2
Ice	10 lbs.	20 lbs.	30 lbs.
Lemonade concentrate, 6 oz. cans, thawed and undiluted	4	8	12
Pineapple concentrate, 6 oz. cans, thawed and undiluted	4	8	12
Water	6 cups	12 cups	18 cups
Ginger ale (33.8 oz. bottle)	2	4	6
Tonic water (28 oz. bottle)	1	2	3
Champagne (25.4oz. bottle)	1	2	3

Sparkling Luau Punch

On the morning of the rehearsal dinner, chill the ginger ale, tonic water, and champagne.

Using the five-gallon bucket, combine the undiluted and thawed concentrates and water and mix well (*do not* add ginger ale). Cover and return to refrigerator until ready to leave for the dinner site.

On the way to the dinner site, stop and pick up the required amount of ice. Arrive at dinner site no earlier than 30 minutes prior to the dinner.

Pour ice into punch fountain.

Pour ginger ale, tonic water, and champagne into concentrate mixture and mix well.

Pour finished punch into punch fountain and turn on the fountain.

Help the dessert person plate up the desserts and set them at each place setting above the napkin.

Monitor fountain during dinner and refill as needed.

At the end of dinner, assist with clean up.

Luau Dining Room (25 guests)

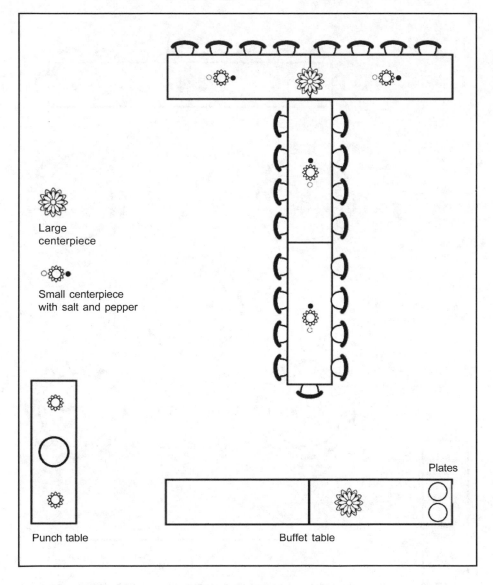

Large
centerpiece

Small centerpiece
with salt and pepper

Punch table

Plates

Buffet table

Luau Dining Room (50 guests)

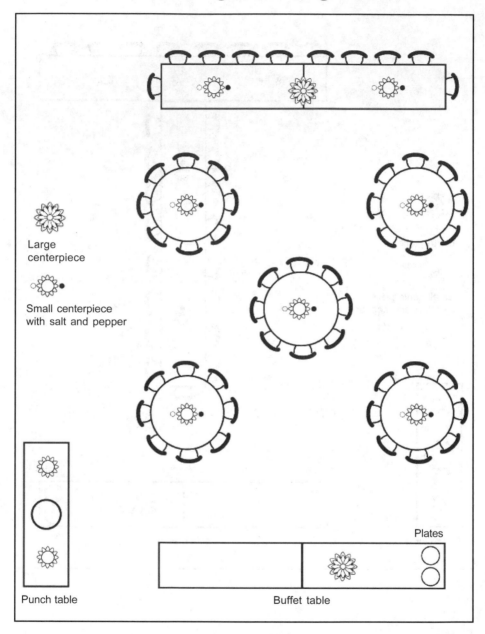

Large centerpiece

Small centerpiece with salt and pepper

Punch table

Plates

Buffet table

Luau Dining Room (75 guests)

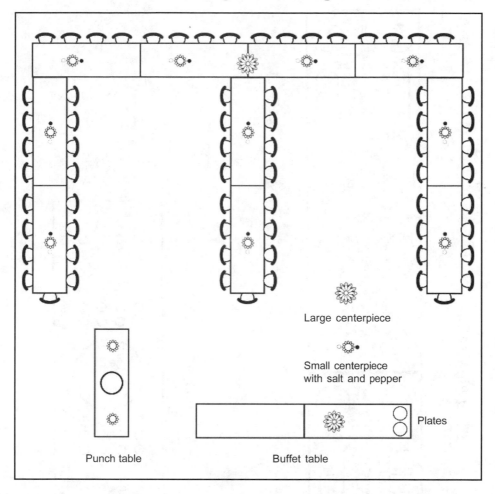

Large centerpiece

Small centerpiece
with salt and pepper

Plates

Punch table

Buffet table

Luau Individual Place Setting

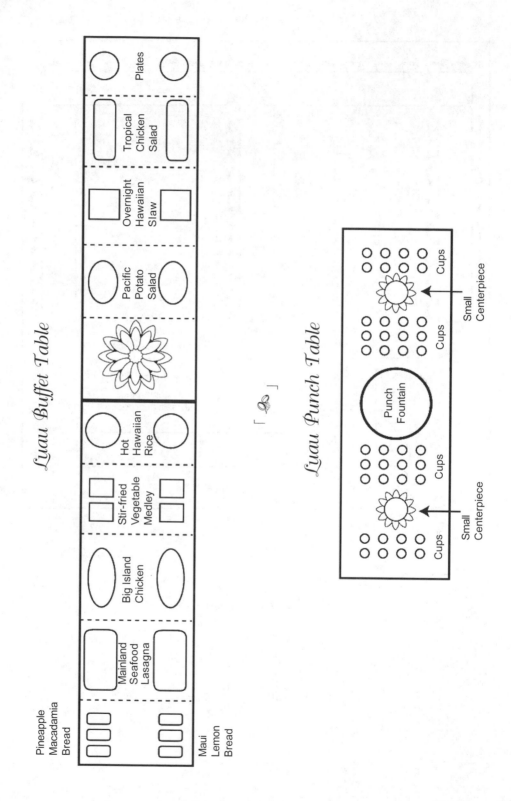

Luau Buffet Table

Plates — Tropical Chicken Salad — Overnight Hawaiian Slaw — Pacific Potato Salad — Hot Hawaiian Rice — Stir-fried Vegetable Medley — Big Island Chicken — Mainland Seafood Lasagna — Pineapple Macadamia Bread — Maui Lemon Bread

Luau Punch Table

Cups — Punch Fountain — Small Centerpiece — Cups — Cups — Small Centerpiece — Cups

 *Appendix*

Recipe Conversions

The ingredient amounts indicated in each recipe have been calculated to feed groups of varying sizes. However, you can easily customize the recipes to fit the number of guests you plan to serve by halving, doubling, or tripling the amounts.

Common Kitchen Equivalents

Standard	Equivalent	Liquid Equivalent
One pinch or dash	1/16 teaspoon	
3 teaspoons	1 tablespoon	1/2 ounce
4 tablespoons	1/4 cup	2 ounces
1/3 cup	5 tablespoon + 1 teaspoon	
1/2 cup	8 tablespoons	4 ounces
1 gill	1/2 cup	4 ounces
1 cup	16 tablespoons	8 ounces
2 cups	1 pint	16 ounces
2 pints	1 quart	32 ounces
4 quarts	1 gallon	
8 quarts	1 peck	
4 pecks	1 bushel	
16 ounces	1 pound dry measure	

tsp. = teaspoon

Tbsp. = tablespoon

oz. = ounce

c = cup

pt. = pint

qt. = quart

bu = bushel

lb. = pound

Metric Conversion Chart

US	Canadian	Australian
1/4 tsp.	1 mL	1 ml
1/2 tsp.	2 mL	2 ml
1 tsp.	5 mL	5 ml
1 Tbsp.	15 mL	20 ml
1/4 cup	50 mL	60 ml
1/3 cup	75 mL	80 ml
1/2 cup	125 mL	125 ml
2/3 cup	150 mL	170 ml
3/4 cup	175 mL	190 ml
1 cup	250 mL	250 ml
1 quart	1 liter	1 litre

Index